The Thinking Classroom

Learning and Teaching in a Culture of Thinking

Shari Tishman
Harvard University

David Perkins
Harvard University

Eileen Jay
Harvard University

Allyn and Bacon
Boston • London • Toronto • Sydney • Tokyo • Singapore

Vice President and Publisher: Nancy Forsyth
Editorial Assistant: Christine Nelson
Production Administrator: Susan McIntyre
Editorial-Production Service: Ruttle, Shaw & Wetherill, Inc.
Cover Administrator: Suzanne Harbison
Composition Buyer: Linda Cox
Manufacturing Buyer: Louise Richardson

Library of Congress Cataloging-in-Publication Data

Tishman, Shari.
   The thinking classroom: learning and teaching in a culture of
thinking / Shari Tishman, David Perkins, and Eileen Jay.
     p. cm.
   Includes bibliographical references and index.
   ISBN 0-205-16508-7
   1. Thought and thinking—Study and teaching. 2. Classroom
environment. I. Perkins, David N. II. Jay, Eileen (Eileen S.)
III. Title.
LB1590.3.T55 1995
370.15'2—dc20   94-11003
                                                      CIP

Printed in the United States of America

10 9 8 7 6 5 4   99

About the Authors

Shari Tishman is a research associate at Project Zero, Harvard Graduate School of Education, and has been involved in the thinking skills movement for over a decade. She consults with educators nationally and internationally regarding the development of thinking-centered instruction and policy and has published widely in the area of critical thinking and its teaching. Among her publication credits is "Thinking Connections," a program for integrating the teaching of thinking with subject matter instruction, which she codeveloped with Perkins and others.

David Perkins was a founding member of Project Zero at the Harvard Graduate School of Education and has served as its codirector since 1971. The Project encompasses cognitive development and cognitive skills in both humanistic and scientific domains. He has conducted long-term programs of research and development in the areas of teaching and learning for understanding, creativity, problem solving, and reasoning in the arts and sciences, as well as everyday life. Among his many publications are *The Mind's Best Work, Teaching Thinking: Issues and Approaches, Knowledge as Design* and *Smart Schools: From Educating Memories to Educating Minds*.

Eileen Jay is a researcher at Project Zero, Harvard Graduate School of Education, investigating new approaches to the teaching of thinking. She has done extensive research on problem finding, studying the disposition to pose problems and its relationship to creativity. Her work includes classroom research and curriculum development on the nature of science and scientific inquiry. She is an author and consultant with recent publications in the areas of problem finding, the teaching of thinking, and the nature of science.

Contents

Acknowledgments

Many of the ideas expressed in *The Thinking Classroom* were developed under a series of grants from the John T. and Catherine D. MacArthur Foundation. We are grateful to the foundation for its assistance, and for its commitment to encouraging innovative, cross-disciplinary research around the teaching of thinking. Also present in this book are ideas drawn from research and development work supported by the Spencer Foundation and the Pew Foundation. To these institutions, too, we are grateful.

We thank Albert Andrade, Katherine Cress, and Jane Gaughan for their thoughtful critiques of an earlier draft of this book; their comments helped us to make a number of important improvements. We also thank our editor at Allyn & Bacon, Nancy Forsyth, for her support and counsel.

Not surprisingly, a book that emphasizes the importance of a culture of thinking grows out of a culture of thinking itself. Project Zero at Harvard University is just such a culture, and we are pleased to be a part of it. In particular, we are grateful to Heidi Goodrich, Rebecca Simmons, and Chris Unger, three colleagues at Project Zero with whom we work particularly closely, for their participation in a community in which the ideas expressed in this book can grow and flourish.

▶ 1

Introduction: The Idea of a Culture of Thinking

Schools are places of culture. Not only in the sense that they introduce students to great intellectual achievements, but also in their sense of community, their spirit of common enterprise. Spend a little time in any classroom and you will instinctively sense it—a particular culture of teaching and learning. It is evident in the way students and teachers interact, in their expectations of one another, their common ways of talking, their shared understanding of what is acceptable, what is interesting, what is valuable.

Naturally, not all classrooms have the same cultural feel: some are rigid, others open; some value answers, others questions. But every classroom has a culture of some sort, and this cultural aspect of education is one of the things that makes the experience of schooling so much greater than the sum of its parts.

This book is about teaching thinking. In particular, it is about how to transform the culture of the classroom into a culture of thinking. The purpose of teaching thinking is to prepare students for a future of effective problem solving, thoughtful decision making, and lifelong learning. This book is about how to achieve these goals.

So why focus on the culture of the classroom? In recent years there has been lots of talk in education about thinking skills—critical thinking skills, creative thinking skills, problem-solving skills, and the like. To be sure, thinking skills are important. Crucial, in fact. But simply having a skill is no guarantee that you will use it. In order for skills to become part of day-to-day behavior, they must be cultivated in an environment that values and sustains them. Just as children's musical skills will likely lay fallow in an environment that doesn't encourage music, learners' thinking skills tend to languish in a culture that doesn't encourage thinking.

A CULTURE OF THINKING

What does it mean to talk about a culture of thinking? Broadly, the notion of culture refers to the integrated patterns of thought and behavior that bind together members of a group. To draw attention to the cultural aspect of a community is to point to things that are shared by most or all community members. For example, community members may share a language or a vernacular, similar values and ideals, similar habits and expectations, a sense of identity, like-minded ways of interpreting the world.

Culture is an aspect of large, national communities, such as French culture, Xhosa culture, or Mexican culture. It can also be an aspect of smaller communities, bound together by factors other than race or geography. For example, one might talk about the culture of youth, the culture of education, the culture of small-town America, the culture of classic car collecting. To talk about a *classroom culture of thinking* is to refer to a classroom environment in which several forces—language, values, expectations, and habits— work together to express and reinforce the enterprise of good thinking. In a classroom culture of thinking, the spirit of good thinking is everywhere. There is the sense that "everyone is doing it," that everyone—including the teacher—is making the effort to be thoughtful, inquiring, and imaginative, and that these behaviors are strongly supported by the learning environment.

SIX DIMENSIONS OF A CULTURE OF THINKING

This book explores six dimensions of good thinking and how to take a cultural approach to teaching them. These six dimensions are:

1. a language of thinking
2. thinking dispositions
3. mental management
4. the strategic spirit
5. higher order knowledge
6. transfer

A language of thinking has to do with the terms and concepts used in the classroom to talk about thinking, and how the language used by the teacher and students in the classroom can work to encourage more high-level thinking.

Thinking dispositions have to do with students' attitudes, values, and habits of mind concerning thinking, and what the classroom environment can do to promote productive patterns of intellectual conduct.

Mental management (sometimes called metacognition) concerns students' thinking about their own thinking processes, and how the classroom culture can encourage students to take control of their thinking more creatively and effectively.

The strategic spirit is a special kind of attitude encouraged in a culture of thinking, one that urges students to build and use thinking strategies in response to thinking and learning challenges.

Higher order knowledge looks beyond the factual knowledge of a subject matter and focuses on knowledge and know-how about the ways of solving problems, using evidence, and doing inquiry in a discipline.

Transfer concerns applying knowledge and strategies from one context to another, and exploring how seemingly different areas of knowledge connect to one another.

TEACHING THINKING: AN "ENCULTURATION" APPROACH

Culture-based teaching, or "enculturation," involves somewhat different teaching techniques than the topic-based teaching techniques that might be used to teach students factual knowledge about the metric system, for example, or the nineteenth-century China trade.

Think about any culture you are part of—an extended family culture, an ethnic culture, an interest-based culture like car collecting or square dancing. Enculturation into any of these kinds of communities typically occurs in four broad ways.

To begin with, you are exposed to *models* of the culture—people who are cultural "insiders" or experts and engage in the kinds of activities that are central to the culture. Cultural models provide examples, or illustrations. For instance, a cultural model of an extended family would be a family member acting in a familylike way (acting brotherly or maternally, for example). A model of a culture of thinking would be an example of someone or something demonstrating good thinking practices.

A second way enculturation happens is through *explanation:* someone or something straightforwardly explains a key piece of culturally important knowledge. For instance, in the culture of square dancing you might be directly taught certain dance steps (accompanied, most likely, by square dancing models—examples of people square dancing). Explanation in a culture of thinking might include direct explanation about specific thinking tactics (such as the tactic of brainstorming), as well as direct transmission of important information pertaining to good thinking (information about the concept of evidence, for example).

A third way enculturation occurs is through *interaction* with other members of the cultural community. For example, spending time talking to car buffs is a good way to become initiated into the culture of car collecting. In a culture of thinking, interaction involves thinking along with others— cooperative problem solving, for instance, or participation in thinking-oriented discussions.

Finally, enculturation occurs through *feedback*. Feedback occurs when members of a community provide evaluative or corrective information about people's behavior within that community. Feedback can be explicit and overt, for example through point-blank criticism. Or it can be tacit and embedded in community values and traditions. Feedback in a culture of thinking occurs when people receive positive or negative input from the culture about their thinking processes. An example of such feedback would be when a teacher praises a student for providing sound supporting reasons for a particular point of view, or when a student's peers comment on the strengths and weaknesses of the student's solution to a problem. Feedback also includes traditional assessments and examinations, because students experience these things as behavior-shaping judgments about their intellectual performances.

Some forms of traditional assessment do indeed convey useful feedback, for example when they provide information that helps students revise or improve their work. But often traditional assessments fail to convey useful feedback about students' thinking: they simply judge students' thinking as right or wrong, without revealing what is right or wrong about it. In a culture of thinking, feedback should be informative and learning-centered. That is, it should provide students with useful information about their thinking behaviors—information that can help them learn how to think better.

In sum, there are four powerful cultural forces in the thinking classroom: models, explanation, interaction, and feedback. How do these forces play out in terms of the six dimensions of thinking mentioned earlier? Here is an example.

Recall that one of the six dimensions of good thinking is called "the strategic spirit." Part of cultivating students' strategic spirit involves teaching them to use thinking strategies when tackling important thinking challenges, for instance, decision making. Imagine, then, a sixth-grade teacher who wants to cultivate students' strategic spirit by helping them think strategically about decision making.

The first thing she (or he) does is straightforwardly explain to students the importance of strategic decision making (cultural force: explanation). As a way of making the explanation vivid, she describes a situation in which she herself used a decision-making strategy to help decide which kind of car to buy (cultural force: models).

She then teaches students a simple decision-making strategy, one that tells them to look for creative options, and to think carefully about pro and con reasons for their choice. She explains each step of the strategy, and draws a model of it on the blackboard (cultural forces: explanation and models).

Finally, she asks students to work in groups of three and use the decision-making strategy to think through a decision in American history: the colonists' decision to dump tea in Boston Harbor. "Talk among yourselves and pretend you are the colonists," she says. "What are your options? What choice would you make? Why?" (cultural force: interaction). As students work, she circulates the classroom, providing advice and encouragement (cultural force: feedback).

So far, this example illustrates a relatively frontal approach to cultivating thinking, a point-blank lesson that harnesses the four cultural forces. However, culture is pervasive—not just a matter of lessons occasionally taught but how things happen in general. Alert to this, our teacher does not stop with the above and a couple of more lessons on decision making and history; she works to keep the strategic spirit alive around decision making.

- She puts a poster up displaying key ideas about decision making (cultural force: explanation).
- When opportunities arise, she explains and demonstrates strategic approaches to decision making concerning historical events—Pearl Harbor, the dropping of the first atomic bomb (cultural forces: explanation and models).
- She encourages strategic decision making in whole class settings ("let's use this strategy to decide between these field trips"), small group settings ("decide strategically which topic you would like to research"), and individual settings ("each of you list some options and make a strategic decision about your essay topic"), across the subject matters (cultural force: interaction).
- She involves students in some decisions about what they will study next, sharing her own thoughts and thinking strategically with them (cultural forces: modeling and interaction).
- From time to time, she gives direct process feedback about whether students have considered lots of options, whether they've developed

reasons for options, and similar criteria for good decision making (cultural force: feedback).

- She gives process advice—"Maybe we should look for more options here"—which informs by redirecting rather than by criticizing (cultural force: feedback).

This does not happen all at once or all the time in any one subject matter. It is occasional, opportunistic, and varied. Through such tactics, our teacher tries to keep the strategic spirit alive around decision making.

Examples such as this one, in which the cultivation of students' thinking is discussed in terms of the four cultural forces, occur in many places in this volume, for each of the six dimensions of thinking.

HOW THIS BOOK IS ORGANIZED

Readers who have already perused the Contents know that the chapters in this book are organized in pairs. For each dimension of thinking, a first chapter provides an overview and explanation of the core ideas of the dimension, and a companion chapter immediately following it provides "pictures of practice"—examples and illustrations of the thinking dimension in practice in the classroom. For those interested in trying some of these ideas out in their classrooms, the "pictures of practice" chapters also offer guidelines for instruction. Readers who are not at present looking for specific instructional tactics may choose to skim parts of the "pictures of practice" chapters.

2

The Language
of Thinking

> **Language of Thinking:** *1. The words in a language that refer to mental processes and mental products. 2. Words that describe and evoke thinking.*

What is the difference between a laugh and a giggle? Between a chortle and a chuckle? A cackle and a guffaw? The sound of human amusement comes in many forms. And even though in a broad sense each of the above words is synonymous with the word *laugh,* it is more accurate to say that each one has its own special meaning, its own unique associations of sounds and innuendos.

Laughter is important. We enjoy it, and when others laugh, it can be important to hear exactly what kind of laugh it is. Because laughter can signify many things: pleasure, love, friendship, malice, playfulness, nervousness, even pain. This is not to say that each individual instance of laughter has multiple meanings. On the contrary; nothing is so simple and simply pleasing as a heartfelt laugh. But when you consider as a whole all the varieties of laughter—all their different meanings and intents—the phenomenon of human laughter is astonishingly complex.

When a phenomenon is complex, it tends to have many words to describe it. So it is with laughter. Another such human phenomenon, even more complex and copiously named, is thinking.

Thinking. It's what you do in your head, right? Well, yes. But choosing the words to identify precisely what kind of thinking you (and others) are doing can be quite a challenge. The English language contains literally hundreds of ways to name and describe different kinds of thinking. To see how this is so, take a moment to consider the meaning of these six words:

guess	surmise	assume
suppose	presume	speculate

Broadly, all these words describe a similar kind of thinking process. They all mean: *to form an opinion based on inconclusive evidence.* More precisely, however, each word marks a subtle and important difference in the relationship of evidence to opinion. For example, the word *guess* suggests no or weak evidence, whereas the word *suppose* suggests an opinion based on a moderate amount of evidence. The word *surmise* suggests a stronger, inferential (but still not irrefutable) link to evidence. When these words are attached to statements, they each qualify the information content of the statement in a different way.

There are two main reasons for having so many words to describe thinking. The first is that it is important for language to provide cues to tell us how statements should be evaluated or interpreted. For example, if you read in a magazine that white bread causes cancer, and you're in the middle of eating a sandwich, it helps if the magazine text also includes words to describe the thinking *behind* the statement—words that tell you, for instance, whether the statement is a speculation, a hypothesis under investigation, or an inference based on carefully gathered evidence.

The second reason we have a rich vocabulary of thinking is that words teach concepts and thereby create paths for thinking to follow. The more ways of describing thinking that are available to language learners, the more paths learners will have along which to direct their thinking. Having lots of words to describe precise differences in kinds of thinking makes it possible to *think* more precisely.

WHAT IS THE LANGUAGE OF THINKING?

The language of thinking consists of all the words and modes of communication in a natural language that refer to thinking processes and thinking products. These include words like *think, believe, guess, conjecture, hypothesis, evidence, reasons, estimate, calculate, suspect, doubt,* and *theorize,* to name just a few. (For a more complete list of a language of thinking vocabulary, see the vocabulary list on pages 11 and 12.) These words describe either a *kind* of mental activity (e.g., guessing, estimating, theorizing), or a *product* of mental activity (e.g., a guess, estimate, theory).

We all use language of thinking terms all the time, for example when we say things like: "I *guess* that's the right phone number," "I *believe* we are in the midst of a major change in world politics," and "that's an interesting *conclusion.*"

One place where you might expect to hear lots of language of thinking is in the school classroom. After all, school is a place where we expect thinking to occur. And some classrooms do indeed seem to have a rich language of thinking; one hears teachers and students use plenty of intellectually evocative words like *reasons, conclusion, evidence,* and *opinion.* But in other classrooms the language of thinking is sparser, and teachers and students tend to use broad words like *think, guess,* and *feel* to cover a wide range of more precise cognitive processes.

In terms of the quality of students' thinking, does it really make a difference whether the classroom language of thinking is rich or sparse? Judge for yourself. Here are two examples of language of thinking in the classroom. The first example is a dialogue between a fourth-grade teacher and her students. The second example is the same dialogue, recast to reflect a richer language of thinking.

The class has been studying aviation, and students have just finished reading about the life of Amelia Earhart. The language of thinking words used by teacher and students are emphasized in bold.

Teacher: Amelia Earhart disappeared somewhere over the Pacific Ocean in 1937; no remains from a plane crash have ever been found. People have said many different things about what happened to Amelia and her plane. What do *you* think happened? Does anyone have any **ideas** about why she disappeared?

Student #1: Maybe her engine blew up.

Teacher: That's one **idea.** Any other **ideas?**

Student #2: I don't **think** her engine blew up; I **think** she just didn't want to come home. Maybe she ran away.

Student #1: Yeah, maybe she's living on a desert island; maybe she landed her plane on purpose on a nice sandy beach somewhere.

Teacher: What makes you **think** she might have got lost "on purpose"?

Student #1: It would be fun, and maybe she had enemies at home.

Teacher: Let's ask the rest of the class; is this a good **guess** about what happened to Amelia Earhart?

Notice that the words used most frequently in this example are "think" and "idea." Used as they are, these words lack specificity, and are broadly construed to cover lots of different kinds of thinking. For example, the first time the teacher uses the word *think,* he is asking students to propose a theory. Later, when he asks students what makes them think that Amelia

Earhart got lost on purpose, he is asking for reasons to *support* a proposed theory. But although he is asking children to do two different things—to propose theories and to give reasons—his language doesn't provide the children with any verbal cues that specify the different kinds of thinking he expects of them.

Here is the same example, rewritten to reflect a much richer language of thinking. Again, the language of thinking vocabulary is in bold.

Teacher: Amelia Earhart disappeared somewhere over the Pacific Ocean in 1937; no remains from a plane crash have ever been found. People have held many different **theories** about what happened. What is your **theory?** Why do you **think** Amelia disappeared?

Student #1: Maybe her engine blew up.

Teacher: That's one **theory.** Is there any **evidence** to support that **theory?**

Student #1: Well. . . . They never found any remains, so when it blew up, the plane probably fell into the ocean.

Teacher: The fact that no remnants were ever found doesn't **contradict** the **theory** that her engine blew up. But I'm not sure it **proves** it. Does anyone else have another **theory?**

Student #2: I don't **think** her engine blew up; I **think** she just didn't want to come home. Maybe she ran away.

Teacher: Is this a **theory** you are **suggesting?**

Student #2: Yeah, I'm **suggesting** it, but it's just a **possibility.** Maybe she's living on a desert island; maybe she landed her plane on purpose on a nice sandy beach somewhere, so she could have a more peaceful life. She was very famous, you know. I **guess** lots of reporters probably bugged her.

Teacher: You give some interesting **reasons** to **support** this **theory**; is there any **evidence** you **know** of—**evidence** that **suggests** that she *did* want to run away from publicity?

Notice that in this latter example, the teacher's language cues and supports very specific patterns of thinking. He explicitly asks the children to propose theories and connects the concept of theory to the concept of supporting evidence, thereby communicating to the class something important about how theories are built. Further, he encourages the children, too, to use language of thinking terminology to more precisely identify their own thinking, such as when he asks a child to clarify whether his statement was intended as a theory. By responding to the student in this way, the teacher is building on the concepts he introduced earlier in the dialogue, and communicates to the student that if he meant his comment as a *theory*, supporting reasons and evidence should also be offered.

A common objection to using a rich language of thinking like the one in the foregoing dialogue is that many students—especially younger students—aren't familiar with the vocabulary words or the concepts behind them, words like *theory, evidence,* and *proof.* But language of thinking vocabulary represents important concepts to *think* with, and we know from experience with language learning in general that concepts and vocabulary are best learned in natural, everyday contexts, such as reading and conversation. So deciding to use a rich language of thinking in the classroom doesn't mean that children must already know the precise definitions of sophisticated words. Rather, it is an effective way to introduce and teach such a language.

A Language of Thinking Vocabulary

Here is a long list of (only some!) language of thinking terms. The length of the list isn't meant to intimidate: there is no expectation that teachers will or should use *all* these words in instruction. We offer a long list for two reasons. First, it gives a view of the range and scope of the language of thinking terms in relatively common usage (most readers will know the meaning of every single one of these words). Second, the list is a helpful resource for educators who want to enrich the language of thinking in their classrooms, and we refer to the list in several of the activities described in the next chapter.

A Language of Thinking Vocabulary

advance	concede	deny	evidence
affirm	conclude	derive	examine
allege	confirm	detect	explain
analyze	conjecture	determine	explore
appraise	consider	disbelieve	fathom
appreciate	construe	discern	glean
apprehend	contemplate	disclaim	grasp
ascertain	contend	discover	grope
assert	contradict	discredit	guess
assess	contravene	discriminate	hypothesize
assume	convince	dispute	imply
attest	corroborate	dissect	infer
aver	criticize	dissent	inquire
believe	decide	divine	inspect
calculate	declare	doubt	interpret
cerebrate	deduce	elucidate	intuit
claim	define	entertain	investigate
cognize	deliberate	establish	judge
comprehend	demonstrate	estimate	justify

know	process	recollect	submit
maintain	profess	reflect	suggest
meditate	propose	remember	suppose
muse	propound	research	surmise
observe	prove	resolve	survey
opine	question	review	suspect
perceive	rate	ruminate	theorize
ponder	realize	scrutinize	think
posit	reason	solve	understand
postulate	rebut	speculate	verify
presume	reckon	state	warrant
probe	recognize	study	weigh

Amazing, isn't it, the range of words there are to describe the life of the mind?

WHY IS A LANGUAGE OF THINKING IMPORTANT?

While there are plenty of reasons to support the view that good thinking is cultivated by exposure to a rich linguistic environment, here is an interesting paradox. Classroom texts—at all levels, even college texts—use very few words from the above list. Yet research shows that even children in the early elementary grades have acquired the necessary conceptual apparatus to understand the meanings of many of these terms, even if they haven't yet been introduced to the actual vocabulary word (Olson & Astington, 1990). For example, although fourth graders might not be familiar with the word *confirm,* they are familiar with the conceptual components that the concept of *confirm* is built out of (i.e., the concept of true and false beliefs and the concept of reasons for believing something).

Why is the linguistic environment of schools so sparse? Perhaps one reason is a well-meaning but misguided desire to make learning easy. Educators and textbook writers tend to simplify language, in order to make the presentation of difficult material more attractive and accessible to children. Yet doing this prevents learners from receiving the important linguistic cues they need, in order to guide and manage their own thinking. How, exactly, does the language of thinking help students to think better? Here are two important ways.

1. The language of thinking helps students organize and communicate their own thinking more precisely and intelligently. Words are precision instruments. They create categories to think with—categories to apply not only to received information, but also to one's own thoughts. For example, it is a small step from learning that other people's theories—for instance the theories of scientists or historians—involve claims and assumptions, to an awareness that one's own thinking often takes the form of theory making, and likewise calls for the finding of evidence and the giving of reasons.

2. **The language of thinking communicates and reinforces standards for thinking.** Words tell you what kinds of thinking are appropriate when. For example, earlier, in the second version of the Amelia Earhart dialogue, recall how the teacher used the word "theory" to communicate that there are certain standards of thinking associated with theory making—standards that include the seeking of evidence and the giving of reasons. Using certain words with students signals expectations about what is sometimes called "the level of discourse."

Here is another example. Suppose you are discussing *Huckleberry Finn* in English class. If you simply ask your students why they think Huck ran away, you will probably get a brief, one-sentence response (something like, "Pap beat him"). But if you set standards for students' responses in the phrasing of your questions—for example, by asking them for *reasons* to support their view, by asking them to *consider alternative interpretations*, by asking them to *analyze* Huck's motives, and so on—you are raising the level of discourse, and are thus more likely to elicit detailed, thoughtful responses.

THE BOTTOM LINES: INCORPORATING A LANGUAGE OF THINKING INTO THE CULTURE OF THE CLASSROOM

Suppose you want to make a language of thinking a part of your own school or classroom culture. What are the elements of success? Recall the four cultural forces mentioned in the introduction: models, explanation, interaction, feedback. These are four powerful ways in which a culture teaches, or enculturates, patterns of good thinking. Models are examples or demonstrations of good thinking in practice. Explanation concerns the direct transmission of information relevant to good thinking. Interaction involves the active use of good thinking practices with other community members. And feedback refers to informative input by community members about the soundness of their thinking practices.

These four cultural forces can all be put to use in cultivating the language of thinking in the classroom. To begin with, *modeling* a language of thinking means incorporating examples and demonstrations of language of thinking words and concepts into regular classroom practice. For instance, using lots of language of thinking words in class and pointing them out in newspapers and textbooks are ways of modeling a language of thinking.

Secondly, providing *explanations* in a language of thinking means directly teaching the meaning of language of thinking terminology, along with direct instruction in its use. So, for example, you might explain to students what the word *conclusion* means, and also explain how to appropriately draw their own conclusions and identify the conclusions of others.

Thirdly, culture is an active and interactive phenomenon. Enculturating a language of thinking involves providing lots of opportunities for learners to use language of thinking terms and concepts in their everyday classroom *interactions* with others. This means creating the expectation that students will use these terms in their writing, in their group work with other students, and in speaking with you the teacher.

Finally, providing feedback in a language of thinking means providing students with informative encouragement and guidance around their use of language of thinking terms and concepts. In large part, feedback in a language of thinking happens much the same way feedback occurs in other language learning: through expert rephrasing of novice talk. We saw this in the Amelia Earhart dialogue, when the teacher rephrased what students said to reflect more precise language of thinking concepts. An example of this is when a student says "I think such and such," and a teacher responds by saying, "that's an interesting theory you are proposing." The teacher's response is feedback because the teacher is acknowledging the student's thought, and is, through the use of the word *theory*, communicating information about how to recast the thought more precisely. Other forms of feedback around a language of thinking might include traditional assessments of students' knowledge of language of thinking vocabulary and concepts, in the form of exams or quizzes.

The foregoing points about how the four cultural forces can be put to use in cultivating students' language of thinking are useful as instructional "bottom lines"—checkpoints teachers can use to make sure that the language of thinking is being incorporated into the classroom culture. Here are the four forces, spelled out explicitly as bottom lines. As a rule of thumb, any lesson or activity that touches on at least two of these bottom lines will almost certainly be doing students' thinking some good.

To enculturate a language of thinking, the bottom lines are:

1. Model and exemplify a language of thinking. Use a rich language of thinking regularly in classroom discourse—a language of thinking that includes much of the vocabulary from the list in the previous chapter. Under normal circumstances, "regularly" means every day, in every subject.

2. Provide explanations about the purpose and use of language of thinking terms and concepts. Point to, and discuss, language of thinking words in all sorts of written and verbal material—in textbooks, newspapers, lectures, speeches, news reports, posters, magazine articles, and so on. Encourage students to point to such language, too. (For example, explain the purpose of the word *claim* in a news report that states: "witnesses claim to have seen a blond man running from the scene of the crime".)

3. Encourage interaction. When students are writing, answering questions in class, or talking with you and each other, prompt them to use a rich language of thinking themselves.

4. Ensure encouraging and informative feedback. Support students' efforts to use a language of thinking and provide information about the use of language of thinking words and concepts by recasting student talk more precisely.

Chapter 3 illustrates how these bottom lines play out in actual classroom settings. Called "pictures of practice," the following pages present vignettes and examples that show how teachers use and teach a language of thinking in their classrooms. For educators who wish to try out some of these ideas in their own school or classroom, the following chapter also provides step-by-step guidelines for instruction.

3

The Language of Thinking: Pictures of Practice

It is said that the motto of Michelangelo was "I am still learning." We should be grateful that he didn't feel he had to know everything about sculpture before he took up the chisel!

Learning new ideas and putting them into practice can sometimes have an odd sort of rhythm. On the face of it, one would think that full understanding should come before practice. Look before you leap, so to speak. But in fact, not only is this nearly impossible in many cases, it is also unadvisable. Understanding is often acquired *through* practice. People who have been through training programs or professional schools know this only too well. For instance, how many people come out of a teacher education program really knowing how to teach? It is only by a good measure of hands-on practice that full understanding of what it means to be a teacher genuinely starts to develop.

This commonsense point is offered by way of reassurance to readers who may be interested in trying to do something with the language of thinking in their classroom, but feel uncertain about their grasp on some of the concepts presented in the previous chapter.

The present chapter offers snapshots of a language of thinking in practice. Our purpose is to make vivid some of the more theoretical points made earlier, so that interested educators can identify a strategy for cultivating students' language of thinking that fits with their own instructional interests and settings. This chapter, along with the other "pictures of practice" chapters, is divided into short sections. Here is a preview of the language of thinking sections to come:

1. **Ms. Peters's Poster**
   A story about how a sixth-grade teacher directly introduces the concept and the vocabulary of a language of thinking to her class.

2. **Language of Thinking and Aspects of Teaching**
   An illustration of how the language of thinking can be built into several standard facets of teaching—facets such as presenting information, asking students questions, and conducting classroom discussions.

3. **Albert's Toothache**
   A short dialogue that shows how a second-grade teacher uses rich language of thinking concepts and vocabulary as he leads his young pupils in a book discussion.

4. **Taking the Plunge: Guidelines for Instruction**
   Two different starting points for beginning to teach a language of thinking, each with step-by-step guidelines.

5. **Continuing On: Making a Language of Thinking a Permanent Part of the Classroom Culture**
   Tips and strategies for keeping a language of thinking alive in the classroom, organized by the four cultural forces: models, explanation, interaction, and feedback.

6. **Troubleshooting: Questions and Answers about a Language of Thinking**
   A handful of common concerns about teaching a language of thinking, and what to do about them.

MS. PETERS'S POSTER

Early in the school year Ms. Peters decided she wanted to cultivate a rich language of thinking in her sixth-grade classroom. To this end, she designed a poster with several key language of thinking words on it. But not *too* many words. Ms. Peters put lots of blank spaces on the poster, which she hoped students would fill in, later on, with additional language of thinking words they found on their own. Here is the poster Ms. Peters made. Following it is a sample of the discussion she had with her class, in which she introduced the idea of a language of thinking.

```
┌─────────────────────────────────────────────┐
│           LANGUAGE OF THINKING                │
│                                               │
│   guess          comprehend     question      │
│   hypothesis     decide         imply         │
│   conclude       ──────────     deny          │
│   investigate    demonstrate    ──────────    │
│   ──────────     opinion        doubt         │
│   confirm        justify        interpret     │
│   criticize      ──────────     ──────────    │
│   ──────────     reason         ──────────    │
│   believe        reflect        ──────────    │
│   claim          ──────────     ──────────    │
│   research       verify         ──────────    │
│   ──────────     evidence       ──────────    │
└─────────────────────────────────────────────┘
```

One Monday morning, Ms. Peters tacked the language of thinking poster onto the bulletin board.

"What do all these words have in common?" she asked her students.

They stared hard at the poster, but remained silent.

"These are all words that have to do with *thinking*," she said. "They are words that give us important information about the kind of thinking that is behind things we read or hear. I know this sounds confusing at first, so here is an example. Suppose I say to you, 'All cats are black.' " (Ms. Peters writes this sentence on the board.) "Does my statement give you any information about my thinking?"

No one responded, so Ms. Peters continued:

"Imagine all the different ways I might have said that sentence to give you more information about my thinking. Here are some examples."

Ms. Peters wrote the following sentences on the board, underlining the thinking words.

I guess all cats are black.
I have investigated whether all cats are black.
I am certain that all cats are black.
In my opinion, all cats are black.
Not everyone agrees with the view that all cats are black.

"Notice that each of those sentences says something different about my thinking. The 'thinking' words I use—words like *guess, opinion,* and *investigate*—are clues about the thinking I've done. They tell you something about how sure I am about what I am saying (for example, when I use the words *guess* or *certain*). And they also indicate whether I have thought carefully about what I am saying (like when I use the word *investigate*)."

Students began to look a little more interested. One put up a hand and said, "Like when you guess, you really aren't very sure. And if you're certain, then you're really sure."

"Right, that's the idea," said Ms. Peters. "Now, why does it matter whether you know anything about my thinking, or about the thinking behind any other statements that you read or hear? Because it is *your job* to decide what attitude to take toward what people tell you. Only you can decide whether or not to believe what you read and hear. No one else can do it for you. You have to decide whether what you read or hear is interesting, whether it is intended to persuade you, to inform you, to intrigue you, or to mislead you. Thinking words help you make these kinds of decisions."

Ms. Peters pointed to the poster again. "These words are *precise* words, and they have a special name. They are called *language of thinking* words. They are words that *precisely* describe the kind of thinking behind statements, and words that *precisely* describe the kinds of thinking going on in our own minds."

Ms. Peters paused to take students' questions, then continued.

"Notice that there are lots of blank spaces on the poster. That is because I've only written down a few language of thinking words here. There are many more! And I need you to help me find them. Whenever you hear or read a thinking word, whether it is in class, or outside of school, we'll talk about it and put it up on the poster."

During the next few weeks, the blank spaces on Ms. Peters's poster start to fill up. Ms. Peters makes a point of noting and appreciating language of thinking terminology students use in class, and, whenever possible, writes their words down on the poster. Students catch the spirit. For example, in math period, a student points to the title of a new math workbook called "Exploring Algebra."

"Is 'explore' a language of thinking word?" the student asks.

"Interesting thought," Ms. Peters comments. "What reason do you have for thinking it might be?"

"Well, in this title, the way they use 'explore' means they want you to *think* about algebra—but they want you to think about it in a special way. Like you're supposed to have fun exploring it as if you were an adventurer or something."

Ms. Peters agrees. "Explore" does seem like a language of thinking word. So she writes it on the poster, commends the student for noticing it, and asks the class if anyone has any ideas about what kind of thinking the word *explore* describes. After a bit of discussion and a consultation of the dictionary, the class decides that *explore* is a "mental adventure" word. It describes the kind of thinking you do when you are just starting to think about something new and are about to discover lots of new things. One student points out that sometimes you use the word *explore* when you want to try to look at all sides of something, for example as Ms. Peters used it when she told them to explore new points of view when they were writing stories last week.

Meeting the Bottom Lines

The foregoing chapter discussed four bottom lines for teaching a language of thinking. Here they provide a useful way of analyzing Ms. Peters's story.

Bottom Line: Model a language of thinking. yes ■ no □

Ms. Peters models a language of thinking by using rich language of thinking terms herself. Importantly, she uses precise words for thinking when she asks students questions, and she encourages them to use them in their responses to her questions (this is also a kind of feedback).

Bottom Line: Provide explanations about the purpose and use of language of thinking terms and concepts. yes ■ no □

Ms. Peters uses the poster to straightforwardly explain the concept of a language of thinking and several key language of thinking terms. She also explains the purpose of a language of thinking, emphasizing how it helps people make their thinking more precise and effective.

Bottom Line: Encourage interaction. yes ■ no □

You can't always do everything at once. Ms. Peters's lesson does not incorporate much student/student interaction. However, in the days and weeks to come, as students start to add to the poster, her lessons become more interactive.

Bottom Line: Ensure encouraging and informative feedback. yes □ no ■

It is not Ms. Peters's intent to provide a lot of feedback in this lesson. Her main purpose is to introduce and explain the idea of a language of thinking, although she does provide some positive feedback when she notes and commends students' use of language of thinking terminology and writes their words on the poster.

Following Up: Integrating the Lesson into the Classroom Culture

Ms. Peters keeps the language of thinking poster on the wall throughout the school year: As a visually accessible explanation, it keeps the notion of a language of thinking present in her own and in her students' minds. It also serves as a way to encourage cultural interaction. Ms. Peters encourages students to use the words on the poster in their writing and conversation, and she often refers to the poster during class discussions. For example, when a student makes a particularly stark statement, unqualified by any language of thinking terminology (such as the statement *slavery caused the Civil War*), she asks the student to look at the poster to find words that more precisely represent his thinking. Pointing to the words on the poster, she asks questions like: Are you making an *assumption?* What *reasons* do you have to support your *claim?* How can we *probe* this view further? She also makes a point of continuing to note and commend the students' use of language of thinking words. And, when students say things that aren't expressed in the language of thinking but could be, she rephrases students' word choice conversationally, so that they get informative feedback about how to think and talk more precisely. Thus the cultural force of feedback, not so present at first, comes into play.

Students grow accustomed to the poster. It becomes a game to try to find new words to add to it. Classroom dictionaries and thesauruses get used more than ever, and Ms. Peters has encouraged students to take responsibility for leading class discussion around the new words they find.

LANGUAGE OF THINKING AND ASPECTS OF TEACHING

Almost all teachers make certain instructional moves in the context of their daily teaching activities—moves like presenting information, assigning homework, giving quizzes and tests, asking questions, and conducting class discussions. These instructional practices are everyday aspects of teaching, and they present a convenient framework within which to cultivate the language of thinking. Here is an example of how language of thinking words and concepts can be built into some of the everyday aspects of teaching a history unit.

Aspect: Presenting Information

Imagine you are a teacher who is beginning a unit on the history of the national park system in the United States, and you want to explain to your students how the first national park was founded. As you were planning this unit, you knew that you wanted to introduce many of the language of thinking terms that are central to the study of history—terms such as claim, evidence, belief, and confirm. In the first class, you will be telling students about how Yellowstone National Park, founded in 1872, was the first national park established in the United States and laid the foundation for the national park system as we now know it.

In the book you have read to prepare your presentation, the author (who is a big fan of the national park system) has written: "Our national parks are one of our greatest national treasures." On the lookout for examples of language of thinking concepts, you recognize that this is a *claim*. Rather a strong claim, in fact. So you

- Identify key language of thinking terms in the subject matter,
- Plan when to introduce and define them, and
- Use them often!

plan to tell your students that "some people claim that the national park system is one of our greatest treasures," and use this as an opportunity to introduce and define the word *claim*. Using the dictionary to find ideas about how to define "claim," you decide to tell students that a claim is a statement asserting that something is true. "But," you will go on to say, "just because people *claim* that something is true doesn't mean that it *is* true. Claims are things we must *decide* whether to believe. If we are to believe a claim, it must be supported by good reasons. What reasons," you plan to ask your students, "do you think someone might have for claiming that the national parks are one of the United States' greatest treasures?"

Aspect: Asking Students Questions

Knowing that you want to use language of thinking terms frequently, especially when you ask students questions, you make a list of relevant language of thinking words and keep it on your desk for handy reference. You also make a conscious effort to note where in your questions you would naturally use the words *think* and *feel*.

You know it is easy to use these words broadly when questioning students, because they sound simple and friendly. But you also know they aren't very powerful in terms of eliciting precise patterns of thinking. So

- Plan which language of thinking words you want to emphasize,
- Jot down a few questions ahead of time that include those words, and
- As you question students, try to avoid using overly broad words, like *think* and *feel*.

you try to phrase questions more precisely, and you encourage students to do so as well. For example, rather than ask a student a question like: "Why do you think the national park system started?" You might ask: "For what *reasons* was the national park system started? Can you find reasons in your book? Can you speculate about any other reasons?" As students respond to your questions, you provide feedback by recasting their speech to reflect a richer language of thinking, letting them know by your rephrasing when they could use certain language of thinking words. For example, in response to a student's stated opinion, you ask the student how strong an opinion it is—is it a theory? a guess? an assumption?

Aspect: Conducting Class Discussions

Once you are well into the unit, you plan to conduct a class discussion about the issue of park rules. What sort of behavior should be permitted inside national parks? For example, how long should people be able to stay? Should they be allowed to camp overnight? To hike freely? Who should determine the rules? You decide to organize the discussion quite straightforwardly around language of thinking words and concepts. So you put a few questions about park rules on the blackboard. Next to them you write a list of language of thinking words you've decided to focus on. The words are: claim, believe, evidence, assumption, dispute, research, justify, theorize. You briefly define the words and make dictionaries available for students to consult. Then you begin the discussion by asking students to say something in response to any of the questions on the board. But their response must include at least one language of thinking word from the list. To start the discussion, you give this example. You say: "Suppose I wanted to say something about the question on the board, 'should people be allowed to hike freely?' I might say something like this: 'Most people assume that they should be able to hike freely around a park, but research shows that if people don't stick to trails, delicate vegetation can be killed—vegetation that is an important part of the ecological balance of the park. So in my opinion, the rule about staying on trails is justified.'" After you say this, you ask students if they can identify the language of thinking words you used.

You know that students may feel uncomfortable at first about using some language of thinking terminology. Partly because it may be new to them, and partly because they are afraid of embarrassing themselves by using it improperly. So you encourage risk taking by telling them that you admire verbal bravery—that you'd much rather hear them dare to use a language of thinking word they are not quite sure about, than timidly avoid using the word at all. You provide plenty of positive reinforcement for verbal bravery, and you provide further support by defining language thinking of words in the discussion, whenever it is appropriate to do so.

Meeting the Bottom Lines

The foregoing example shows how the teaching of a language of thinking can extend over several lessons, so it is no surprise that the example as a whole is able to meet all four instructional bottom lines.

Bottom Line: Model a language of thinking. yes ■ no ☐

You (the imaginary teacher in this example) model a rich language of thinking when you are presenting information and take care to alert students to examples of thinking language in texts.

Bottom Line: Ensure explanations about the purpose and use of language of thinking terms and concepts. yes ■ no ☐

You directly explain the use of language of thinking terms and concepts during the discussion of national park rules. You also encourage students to use the dictionary, which is an explanatory tool for language learning.

Bottom Line: Encourage interaction. yes ■ no ☐

You encourage students to use a language of thinking themselves, in their questions to you and to each other, and in class discussions generally.

Bottom Line: Ensure encouraging and informative feedback. yes ■ no ☐

You recast student talk using stronger language of thinking phrasing, thus providing students with contextualized information about which words to use when. Also, you keep in mind that self-consciousness and the fear of embarrassment can prevent students from experimenting with new words, so you provide plenty of positive reinforcement for verbal bravery, and try to make your classroom a safe place for students to take intellectual risks with new language and concepts.

Following Up: Integrating the Lesson into the Classroom Culture

Because this example focuses on several aspects of instruction, it is easy to see how you the teacher can continue to encourage a language of thinking.

You plan to continue to model the use of precise words for thinking, and to point them out to students in the talk and text of others. You will continue to explain language of thinking terms and concepts—both when they arise naturally in regular lessons, and when it makes sense to explicitly design a lesson around them (for example, you are already planning a lesson that explains the concepts of reasons and evidence). You will continue to encourage students to use thinking words; with you and with each other. And you will provide ongoing feedback by rephrasing student talk and by commending verbal bravery around a language of thinking. You also plan to look for and encourage students' use of thinking words in their written work, for example by noting and commending the use of language of thinking terminology in their history essays.

ALBERT'S TOOTHACHE

Educators of younger children may well be asking: Isn't the notion of a language of thinking a bit sophisticated for first, second, and even third graders? The short answer is no. Earlier it was pointed out that even young children have the necessary conceptual apparatus to understand apparently sophisticated language of thinking concepts like *prove, believe, reason,* and *evidence.* Here is a discussion between a second-grade teacher and his students that shows what it can sound like to emphasize these and other language of thinking concepts with young students.

    Mr. Singer has just finished reading a book called *Albert's Toothache* (Williams, 1977) aloud to his class. The story is about a young turtle named Albert, who takes to his bed, claiming to be suffering from a severe toothache. This is very upsetting to Albert's mother and father, and the source of some teasing from his sister and brother, because everybody knows that *turtles don't have teeth!* Finally, Albert's wise grandmother comes to visit, and helps explain Albert's odd complaint to the family. Mr. Singer's classroom dialogue is accompanied by occasional commentary.

Dialog	*Commentary*
Mr. Singer: Albert's mother and father were very upset when Albert took to his bed for a week. Does anyone have any ideas about why they were upset?	
Kathy: They were upset because Albert was sick.	
Jorge: No, they were upset because Albert was *lying.* Because he said he had a toothache. And turtles don't have teeth.	

Kathy: You're wrong! They were upset because he was *sick.*

Mr. Singer: Whoa . . . hold on. Here we have two different opinions about why Albert's parents were upset. Let's examine both opinions, and decide which one to believe. Can anyone think of any reasons in favor of either of these views? For example, what reasons might there be to believe that Albert's parents were upset because he was sick?

Notice that Mr. Singer links the notion of opinion, *or* view, *to the idea that opinions need to be accompanied by reasons. This communicates to students that they need to look for* **reasons** *to believe things.*

Kathy: Well, my parents get upset when I'm sick. *Anyone's* parents get upset when kids are sick.

He continues to reinforce the concept of reasons . . .

Mr. Singer: So are you saying that a *reason* in favor of the view that Albert's parents were upset because Albert was sick is that all parents get upset when their children are sick.

Kathy: Yeah.

Mr. Singer: What are other people's views? Is that a good reason?

. . . and encourages students to evaluate reasons, to decide whether or not they are good reasons.

Jorge: No. Because they didn't *believe* he was sick. So they couldn't get upset about that.

Mr. Singer: This is a very interesting discussion. At first I thought Kathy's view might be right, that Albert's parents were upset because they thought Albert was sick. But now that I think harder about it, I find I want to **reconsider** things—I'm starting to see other points of view. How can we **decide?** What can we do to **investigate** this situation further? *(The class is silent.)*

Here Mr. Singer models something very important for his students: He shows them that good thinking (or, in more poetic terms, the search for truth), often involves **reconsidering things and changing your mind.** *Mr. Singer is not afraid to show his students that he doesn't know the correct answer. Rather, he is communicating to the class that everyone present—including himself—is a partner in the pursuit of well-reasoned opinions.*

Mr. Singer: I have an idea. Let's look at the pictures in the book. Maybe they will give us a **clue** about whether Albert's parents really thought he was sick. *(Mr. Singer slowly flips through the pages of the book, holding the pictures up for students to see.)*

Lily: Wait, stop! There's a picture of Albert's mother putting a cloth on Albert's forehead. She wouldn't be doing that if she didn't think he was sick.

Mr. Singer: Aha! You're a good detective, Lily. You've found some **evidence.** Does anyone know what the word *evidence* means? *(No one responds, so Mr. Singer goes on.)* Evidence is a *sign* that supports an opinion. For example, I might have the opinion that Kathy had a tuna fish sandwich for lunch. But someone might disagree with me, and think that Kathy had peanut butter and jelly for lunch, instead. To show that my opinion is correct, I need to find **evidence.** I need to support my opinion by finding signs, or clues. Now, suppose that Kathy is not in the room. But her lunch box is. I look inside it and I find an empty sandwich wrapper in her lunch box that smells like tuna fish. Or, suppose I called Kathy's father, and he told me he had packed a tuna sandwich in Kathy's lunch box that morning. These things are **evidence** to support my opinion that Kathy ate tuna fish for lunch. *(Mr. Singer continues the discussion, relating it to* Albert's Toothache, *and students continue to look for* ***evidence*** *for their views by examining the pictures in the book. Mr. Singer makes sure to keep the word evidence, and other related language of thinking words, alive in the discussion.)*

When Mr. Singer was planning this lesson, he had hoped to lead the discussion around to the concept of evidence. He feels more comfortable when he plans things out in detail, ahead of time. So before class, he used the dictionary to help him find a way of defining the word evidence *in a way that would make sense to his students. He had even worked out in his head the example of Kathy and the tuna fish sandwich.*

Meeting the Bottom Lines

Mr. Singer's intent was to embed language of thinking terms and concepts in a regular class discussion. In doing so, he mainly addresses the "modeling" and "interaction" bottom lines, although he touches on the other bottom lines, too.

Bottom Line: Model a language of thinking. yes ■ no ☐

Mr. Singer models a rich language of thinking throughout his discussion of *Albert's Toothache* by using words like *reasons, evidence,* and so on.

Bottom Line: Provide explanations about the purpose and use of language of thinking terms and concepts. yes ■ no ☐

Although his primary intent was to model language of thinking words and encourage their use, Mr. Singer took care to directly instruct students in the meaning of a word that might not be familiar to them—the word *evidence*.

Bottom Line: Encourage interaction. yes ■ no □

This is Mr. Singer's main purpose, and he achieves it. In the context of a regular class discussion he helps students to understand and use key language of thinking terms like *reasons* and *evidence*.

Bottom Line: Ensure encouraging and informative feedback. yes ■ no □

Mr. Singer blends modeling with contextualized feedback by recasting what students say to reflect a richer language of thinking. For example, he commends Lily for finding a reason to believe that Albert's parents truly thought Albert was sick, and rephrases what Lily said as "finding evidence."

Following Up: Integrating the Lesson into the Classroom Culture

There are many ways Mr. Singer can continue to encourage a language of thinking in his classroom. He plans to continue to model it, by continuing to use the terminology he has stressed in this lesson. He also plans to straightforwardly explain some further language of thinking concepts. For example, he plans to conduct a lesson around the concept of *belief*, in which he will talk about what it means to believe something, and what it means to have good reasons for what you believe. And of course, he plans to continue to encourage students to use language of thinking terminology in class discussions—with him and with each other.

TAKING THE PLUNGE: GUIDELINES FOR INSTRUCTION

If you find the idea of a language of thinking powerful, you may be interested in trying it out in your own classroom. Beginnings are tough: It's almost always hard to bring a new idea or focus into the classroom, particularly a big, pervasive idea like the language of thinking. You may have a clear vision about how you personally could best get started. If so, by all means pursue it. If you're less sure, here are two possible instructional "plunge points"—points of departure for introducing the idea of a language of thinking to your students.

To begin, read over plunge points 1 and 2 below. Decide which one will work best in your own setting, then follow the steps as you would a regular lesson.

Plunge Point #1

1. Reread the first example in this chapter, "Ms. Peters's Poster," and use it as a guide for designing your own lesson.

2. Make a poster with several language of thinking words on it and several blank spaces for students to fill in later (like Ms. Peters's poster). Some resources that can be helpful in selecting the words for the poster include the list of language of thinking words given earlier, a dictionary, or a thesaurus. Make sure that you are prepared to give easy-to-understand definitions for the words on the list. *Don't be afraid to challenge your students with language of thinking words that sound difficult.* Research has shown that even young students typically surpass teacher expectations concerning their grasp of language of thinking terms and concepts (Olson and Astington, 1991).

3. Read how Ms. Peters introduced the poster to her students and plan to introduce it to your students in a similar way. Make sure to have selected sample sentences like Ms. Peters's "cat" sentences beforehand (or use the "cat" sentences yourself.)

4. Return to the poster frequently throughout the week, in different topics and subject matters. Encourage students to add language of thinking words to the poster. When you hear candidate words yourself in the classroom, ask students whether they think they ought to be on the poster.

5. Reflect. Once you have followed these guidelines, you will have taken the plunge. Consolidate your new, hands-on understanding of a language of thinking by taking a few moments to reflect on your experience.

- Review how your conception of a language of thinking has changed over the past week as you've been putting these ideas into practice. What new insights do you have? What new questions?
- Reflect on your students' understandings. What seem to be their language of thinking strengths and weaknesses?

Plunge Point #2

1. Reread the second example in this chapter, "Language of Thinking and Aspects of Teaching," and use it as a guide for designing your own series of lessons. Identify three instructional occasions in the upcoming week that correspond to the three aspects: (1) an occasion in which you are presenting information, (2) one in which you are asking students questions, and (3) one in which you are conducting a class discussion.

2. For each occasion, reread the subsection that corresponds to it. The boxed text at the beginning of each subsection serves as a step-by-step guide to planning a lesson. For example, when presenting information (aspect one), first, identify key language of thinking terms in the subject matter. Then, plan when to introduce and define them, and so on.

Suggestions for Choosing Language of Thinking Terms and Concepts to Discuss with Students

- Identify mental moves that are key to a subject matter, or key across several subject matters. For instance, looking for evidence is a key move in most subject matters (looking for evidence for an interpretation of a poem, looking for evidence to support a scientific hypothesis, looking for evidence that a political proposal will work). So *evidence* is a good concept to tackle.
- Use the vocabulary list given earlier as a source of ideas for interesting words and concepts.
- Browse a newspaper for ideas (particularly the editorials).
- Choose a few key language of thinking words (e.g., *theory, belief, think, evidence*) and peruse their entries in a thesaurus or dictionary.

CONTINUING ON: MAKING A LANGUAGE OF THINKING A PERMANENT PART OF THE CLASSROOM CULTURE

What comes next, after you have taken the plunge and introduced the language of thinking to your students? To continue to nurture it, simply continue to make use of the four cultural forces: models, explanation, interaction, and feedback. Here are some instructional tactics in each of these areas.

Models of the Language of Thinking

- Use language of thinking terminology regularly with students. Note how often you use broad terms like *think* and *feel* and try to substitute more precise language. For instance, rather than asking students, "what do you think?" ask instead for an opinion, a theory, a speculation, a hypothesis, a conclusion.
- Use language of thinking terms when you talk about your own thinking. For example, identify an inference when you make one, a belief when you express one, a conclusion when you reach one, a doubt when you have one.

- Point out language of thinking terminology in texts and other written materials, and encourage students to do the same. Also, encourage students to notice the *lack* of thinking language, for example when an author makes a questionable statement of fact without qualifying it as a guess, hypothesis, or claim.
- Make language of thinking visual models a permanent part of classroom culture. For instance, keep a poster on the wall with a list of key language of thinking vocabulary. Give students a handout of such a list, which they can add to as they discover new thinking words. Or have a spot for a language of thinking "word of the day" permanently present in a corner of the blackboard.

Explanations of the Language of Thinking

- Directly explain language of thinking concepts and vocabulary. For example, conduct a discussion around the concept of hypothesis. What does the word mean? Does a hypothesis in science differ from one in history? What kinds of hypotheses do we make in everyday life?
- Weave instruction in language of thinking concepts into regular classroom lessons. Often a language of thinking term will be used naturally in the context of a regular lesson. For example, you might be teaching a lesson on the environment and discussing reasons why it is important to recycle paper products. Take the opportunity to explain briefly to students the term *reasons*—what different kinds there are, what makes a good one, and which reasons are particularly important in the case of recycling.

Interaction with the Language of Thinking

- Make the language of thinking a part of everyday classroom discourse. Use precise words for thinking when you talk with students and encourage them to do the same when they talk with you and each other.
- Design cooperative activities that encourage students to use the language of thinking as they work with each other.

Feedback on the Language of Thinking

- Provide students with verbal feedback by rephrasing what they say in class to reflect a richer language of thinking. For example, if a student suggests an idea that is meant as a hypothesis, respond by saying something like: "That's an interesting hypothesis. What evidence do you have for it?"
- Note when students use language of thinking terminology and provide positive reinforcement.

- Encourage students to be linguistically brave and to experiment using language of thinking words and concepts with which they may not initially feel comfortable.
- Use language of thinking terms and concepts on worksheets, tests, and homework assignments, and commend students' use of them in their written work.

Checking Your Progress

One effective method of checking your progress in enculturating a language of thinking is to review your teaching activities related to language of thinking at the end of every week. A weekly chart can help you see how well you are covering the four modes of enculturation: models, explanation, interaction, and feedback. Table 3.1 on page 34 is a sample chart that records some language of thinking activities a teacher might have done during the week. Feel free to design a weekly chart that best suits your teaching objectives.

TROUBLESHOOTING: QUESTIONS AND ANSWERS ABOUT A LANGUAGE OF THINKING

No enterprise is without its challenges and obstacles. This final section identifies some difficulties teachers frequently encounter in cultivating a language of thinking and offers advice about how to surmount them.

Lots of language of thinking words sound kind of . . . well . . . harsh. When you don't take what children say at face value, and instead demand that they give "evidence," or "proof," or "reasons," it sounds like you're saying something negative. Won't this kind of classroom talk hurt children's feelings?

The main reason words like *prove, evidence,* and *reasons,* can sound harsh is that we generally place a premium on people answering questions fully and correctly the first time around, so it seems somehow an insult to be asked to support, or expand on, one's thinking. This is especially true in many traditional school settings, where children are expected to open their mouths only when they *have* the right answer, and aren't encouraged to show any of the thinking involved in pursuing the right answer.

To a large extent, defusing critical-sounding words involves placing explicit value in the classroom on the process of positive criticism, including self-criticism. A simple example of this would be placing a greater value on answers like: "I think such and such is the answer, but I'm not completely

TABLE 3.1 Language of Thinking Weekly Progress Chart

	MONDAY	TUESDAY	WEDNESDAY	THURSDAY	FRIDAY
Models	To model the language of thinking words on the poster, I went through an example of justifying an opinion using the correct terms.	In discussing a Shakespearean sonnet, I asked students to give their *interpretation,* supplying reasons to justify their opinions.	Gave an essay assignment asking students to offer two different interpretations of Macbeth (read last week) with justification.		Introduced new terms for the poster —*evidence* and *assess* —and explained them to the class.
Explanation	Explained language of thinking poster featuring *interpret, opinion, justify, reasons, etc.*				
Interaction	We discussed why using correct words are important. And students tried them out with my help.	We discussed the sonnet, taking down the reasons given for various interpretations.		Had students work in groups to present and debate their interpretations of *Macbeth.*	We discussed what evidence there was for various *Macbeth* interpretations and how to assess the evidence.
Feedback		When students offered an opinion, I reminded them to provide justification and ask for it from each other.		Students gave each other feedback on whether interpretations were justified and reasons adequate.	

certain, because . . . ," or "I think such and such is the answer, and my reasons are . . ." than on an answer like: "Such and such . . . I guess."

When critical discussion, and the language of thinking words associated with it, is seen in the classroom as something positive rather than something to be avoided, the risk of hurting students' feelings (and of students hurting each others' feelings) is greatly reduced. In short, the best way to avoid hurt feelings is to create a classroom culture that actively supports a critical, reason-giving, question-searching, evidence-seeking spirit.

I've looked for language of thinking words in all sorts of classroom materials—textbooks, handouts, quizzes, and supplementary materials—but it's hard to find examples of "thinking" words to point out to students. There don't seem to be many. Am I missing something?

Unfortunately, no. Most classroom materials are pretty sparse when it comes to language of thinking vocabulary because of the well-meaning but misguided notion pointed out earlier—that the language of thinking is too challenging for children. One problem with this view is it keeps children from learning the concepts they need to help them think deeply and precisely. Another problem is that it misrepresents the language–learning process: Children learn new vocabulary very easily when it's used meaningfully in context.

However, traditional classroom materials often do provide opportunities to use a language of thinking, even if thinking words aren't present in the text. What educators can do is look at standard classroom material and ask themselves where language of thinking terminology *should* be used, even if it's not. Remember, virtually all presented information consists of *claims*, which rest on *reasons, evidence, theories,* and so on. So any time materials lend themselves to asking students questions like:

> *Why does the text say such and such . . . ?*
> *How do you know that such and such . . . ?*
> *What reasons are there for such and such . . . ?*
> *What is such and such a claim based on . . . ?*
> *What is your opinion . . . and why . . . ?*

you have an opportunity to use, and encourage, a language of thinking.

Changing how one talks in the classroom is easier said than done. How can I possibly *remember* to use language of thinking vocabulary, when I'm tying hard enough to remember the information I'm presenting to students?

This is a very real concern, and the remedy for it is something that will benefit students, too: *Externalize language of thinking reminders.* Naturally, it's hard to remember to use new words—for adults as well as children. One straightforward solution is Ms. Peters's tactic: Put a language of thinking poster up on the classroom wall. This makes language of thinking words and concepts visible to everyone. The poster can serve as a simple reminder during instruction. It also can be used as a tool to guide discussion ("look at the poster: which words describe the kind of thinking we need to do in this history lesson?"), and to help students with writing ("as you're writing your report, take a look at the poster and see if the words suggest any ways you want to organize or present information. For example, will you need to talk about 'evidence'? Are you making claims in your report that need to be supported by 'reasons'?").

Another way to remember to use language of thinking terminology is to make a short list of the language of thinking words you want to cover in a lesson and keep the list handy on your desk. Whatever method you choose, it is important to remember to be moderate and realistic in your goals. It is quite an accomplishment to simply introduce a few key thinking words into instruction—words, for example, like *claim, reasons,* and *interpret*—and to use them consistently.

Chapters 2 and 3 have emphasized the role of language in helping students to be better thinkers. While language is important, it is of course not all there is to teaching thinking. The goal of teaching thinking is ambitious—to help learners think and act intelligently over the long term. These chapters have argued that language plays an important role in cueing and supporting good thinking. Equally important are students' "thinking dispositions"—their tendencies toward certain patterns of intellectual conduct. Chapters 4 and 5 take up this topic.

▶ 4

Thinking Dispositions

Thinking Dispositions: 1. Inclinations and habits of mind that benefit productive thinking. 2. Ongoing, abiding tendencies in thinking behavior exhibited over time across diverse thinking situations.

Any athlete will tell you that it takes more than raw ability and talent to excel in a sport. Imagine two talented figure skaters of roughly equal ability, both Olympic hopefuls. One skater puts in the requisite practice, following the choreographed routines until she masters them. The other skater, however, is prone to pushing her abilities to the fullest. In her desire for more creative performance, she constantly searches for new, innovative moves to embellish her routine. Her willingness to take risks leads her to create a fresh combination of maneuvers that becomes her signature move. A zest for tinkering with the boundaries of established tradition in a speculative and playful way leads her to experiment with unusual blends of music, mood, and movement. One might say that she is *disposed* to originality, open exploration, and playful risk taking. At the same time, she is disposed to being careful and analytical about her technical execution, through continual self-monitoring of her performance. Her desire for improvement prompts a tendency to persevere and to set goals for advancement.

Abilities and skills alone cannot fully account for human performance. Simply having an ability does not guarantee that one will use it and use it well. In the above example, both skaters displayed equivalent raw ability, yet the second skater enhanced her abilities by using them to greater effect. What is it that was special about the second skater? The distinguishing characteristics were her dispositions to challenge herself, to openly seek new directions, to take risks, to be critical, and to strive for improvement. These characteristics say little about her raw ability but say a lot about how she approached her craft. In general, dispositions represent a person's tendency to use his or her abilities in particular ways and directions. Human performance is comprised of abilities *plus* dispositions.

Thinking is a human endeavor that involves abilities and dispositions. We know that cognitive capabilities play an important role in thinking. However, once again, simply having the ability to think does not mean that one will do it well, or even do it much at all. What sets the good thinker apart from the average thinker is not simply superior cognitive ability. Good thinkers can be distinguished because they use their inherent intellectual powers in productive and probing ways. Good thinkers can be characterized by their thinking dispositions—their abiding tendencies to explore, to inquire and probe into new areas, to seek clarity, to think critically and carefully, to be organized in their thinking, and so on.

Most efforts to teach thinking aim at cultivating thinking skills. Students are taught strategies designed to boost the abilities side of thinking. Unfortunately, students often fail to use the thinking skills they are taught. What can be done to develop the inclination and habit of using thinking skills effectively? One way is through an approach to teaching thinking that stresses the dispositional as well as the abilities side of thinking.

Take the example of Mr. Marcus, a tenth-grade history teacher, who feels that seeing things from other points of view is key to good thinking and reasoning in social studies. However, whenever he presents historical dilemmas and current controversies for discussion, he notices that students only offer arguments for their own side of the case.

In debating Truman's decision to drop the atomic bomb in World War II, Robert maintains, "It had to be done to stop the war. If that hadn't happened, more people would have died in the long run." Meanwhile, Susan gives opposing arguments, "It killed a lot of innocent people. Plus, no one knew what kind of global effect the explosion might have."

Mr. Marcus sees from their spontaneous behavior that they lack the disposition to look for other perspectives on their own. So after each student has the opportunity to present supporting evidence for his or her viewpoint, Mr. Marcus poses the following challenge: "Robert can you try to argue Susan's case? And, Susan, try to put together an argument from Robert's point of view." Although they struggle some, Mr. Marcus finds that the students can indeed argue the other side of the case when asked—they have the ability. It is clear, however, that they do not think to do it on their own. Recognizing this, Mr. Marcus decides to do more than just teach the thinking skills strategy of taking the other side of the case. Instead, he decides to talk about thinking dispositions explicitly.

Mr. Marcus: What Robert and Susan did at first shows us that we are all inclined to look at things from our own point of view. We could say that we have a *disposition* to argue from our own perspective. Can anyone say what I mean by a disposition?

Student #1: It's the way you are. Like when someone has a happy disposition; it means he tends to be happy all the time.

Mr. Marcus: That's right. Dispositions are tendencies or inclinations to behave in certain ways. For example, a person might have a disposition to be considerate or to be argumentative or to sleep late. Tell me what some of your dispositions are. *(Students generate examples such as a disposition to be cheerful, to be polite, to be shy, to eat too much, to play baseball, to be forgetful, to daydream, to stay up late at night.)*

Mr. Marcus: I think you get the idea. Now let's talk about dispositions that have to do with thinking. What are some dispositions that describe your own thinking?

Student #1: Well, my mother says that I am always curious. She says that I never stop asking questions.

Student #2: Most of the time I try to think hard. But sometimes, like when I do a math problem and can't get the answer, I get frustrated and give up.

Student #3: When I make a decision, I have to think of every possibility before I'm ready to decide.

Mr. Marcus: Good. From now on through the term, I want us to pay close attention to our thinking dispositions. We will learn how to recognize them and decide which ones we would like to improve in ourselves. Let's start by listing some of the dispositions we have mentioned so far and deciding whether we think they serve our thinking well or not so well.

Mr. Marcus keeps the idea of thinking dispositions alive throughout the term. He gives his students plenty of practice in thinking skills, such as perspective taking, but he also develops their awareness of their own thinking patterns and tendencies. He is convinced that, if he cultivates the right thinking dispositions inclinations in students, there is a better chance that they will actually use the thinking skills they are taught.

WHAT ARE THINKING DISPOSITIONS?

Thinking dispositions are abiding tendencies toward distinct patterns of thinking behaviors. Just as we can talk about a person's tendency to be friendly or to work hard, we can talk about someone's tendency to be curious or systematic or persistent in their thinking. Good thinkers are disposed to explore, to question, to probe new areas, to seek clarity, to think critically and carefully, to consider different perspectives, to organize their thinking, and so on.

To be disposed toward something means that the person has a tendency to exhibit the behavior over time. So, an important characteristic of thinking dispositions is that they are ongoing, abiding patterns in a person's thinking across many thinking situations. When we say that an individual is a systematic thinker, it means that he or she tends to display systematic thinking in various situations day after day, week after week. Thus, in contrast to abilities which can be assessed at a given point in time, thinking dispositions, by definition, are captured as tendencies that play out over time.

When trying to foster students' thinking dispositions in the classroom, it is important to recognize both that dispositions take time to develop and that they manifest themselves over time. Dispositions cannot be transmitted like a piece of knowledge. Rather they must be cultivated like a plant, with constant nurturing so they can develop fully and grow strong. If you make a commitment to cultivating thinking dispositions, plan to devote attention to them repeatedly over the course of your curriculum. It should be an ongoing, recurring theme rather than an isolated set of lessons.

Likewise, in assessing the progress of students' thinking dispositions, expect that it will take time for dispositions to evince themselves. You may find that students show only incremental change in their patterns of thinking as they gradually incorporate good thinking dispositions. On the other hand, you will have the satisfaction that you are helping them cultivate long-term, sustaining habits of mind.

What is it that makes a person disposed to think well? The origins and underpinnings of thinking dispositions are actually quite diverse. Dispositions can be rooted in habits, policies, motivations, desires, feelings, attitudes, beliefs, understandings, values, or other factors. One may be organized in one's thinking due to habit or due to a conscious policy to be that way. Likewise, one might be disposed to think in an organized fashion due to a belief that it pays off or due to a sense of good form such as an artist might have. At times, dispositions can be driven by almost ritualistic forces; while at other times, dispositions are driven by affective and emotional elements such as attitudes, feelings, motivations, and the like. Normally, multiple influences play a role.

Since dispositions have such complex origins, in the classroom one has to work toward cultivating them on many fronts: promoting alertness, building habits, fostering values, changing attitudes and beliefs, encouraging intrinsic motivation, and so on. For example, suppose you are trying to imbue students with the disposition to be more careful and thorough in their thinking. You would promote alertness to situations where care and thoroughness are needed by discussing with your students when mistakes and omissions are most likely and most costly. You would try to build habits by having them work on careful thinking routinely so that it becomes a well-practiced tendency. Concurrently, you might discuss the value of careful and precise thinking and try to change their attitude that it is too effortful. Moreover, you could motivate students by showing how careful thinking at the outset results in less effort later. By supporting dispositions on several fronts, you lay a better foundation for developing sustained thinking dispositions.

Dispositions are acquired within and influenced by the context of a cultural environment. Everyday experience indicates that dispositions are cultivated all the time through social interaction, a key aspect of enculturation. Take the example of open-mindedness. How might a person develop the attitudes and beliefs that cause him or her to value open-mindedness? Perhaps as a child he or she grew up in a family where members openly discussed and considered alternative points of view, suspended judgment, and changed their views based on new arguments. Influenced by the behavior and values of the surrounding culture, this person developed a disposition to be open-minded.

Likewise, in the classroom, the aim is not so much to teach thinking dispositions as it is to cultivate thinking dispositions within the context of a culture. It would be inadequate to approach the cultivation of dispositions by designing a lesson plan to teach dispositions as one would teach particular content or skills. While explicit lessons about dispositions can be useful, the need for an ongoing, comprehensive, environmental approach cannot be neglected. Thinking dispositions must be enculturated in the context of a culture of thinking. The classroom can become such a culture.

Five Dispositions for Good Thinking

Naturally, countless dispositions for thinking can be identified. The aim here is to get some purchase on a handful of dispositions that foster *good* thinking. After all, not all thinking dispositions necessarily benefit thinking. Some, like the disposition to give up easily in the face of confusion or the disposition to stubbornly ignore instruction, actually block good thinking. Here are five broad, teachable thinking dispositions that contribute powerfully to overall good thinking.

1. The **disposition to be curious and questioning** includes: the urge to question, inquire, wonder, pose problems, probe further, look beyond what's given.

2. The **disposition to think broadly and adventurously** includes: the impulse to explore alternative points of view, be open-minded, be flexible, try new things and ideas, be playful.

3. The **disposition to reason clearly and carefully** includes: the desire to seek clarity, gain understanding, be precise, be thorough, remain alert to possible error.

4. The **disposition to organize one's thinking** includes: the urge to be orderly and logical, be planful, think ahead, approach things in a calculated and methodical fashion.

5. The **disposition to give thinking time** includes: the tendency to devote time and effort to thinking.

These five dispositions represent in capsule form some of the key dispositions for good thinking; however, they are not meant to be exhaustive. Indeed, there are numerous dispositions that one could argue contribute in beneficial ways to good thinking. The important point for this chapter and throughout this volume is that thinking can and should be looked at from a dispositional point of view.

WHY ARE THINKING DISPOSITIONS IMPORTANT?

We have already made the general point that abilities are not enough. In musical terms, abilities and dispositions go together like love and marriage or a horse and carriage. They make up a whole that is greater than the sum of the parts. Still, it is worth looking more specifically at four key reasons why thinking dispositions are important and why they contribute in essential ways to the teaching of thinking.

1. Dispositions are essential to putting good thinking into practice. One can have the ability to do something, such as seeing both sides of the case. However, unless one has the inclination to use it and the sensitivity to recognize when to use it, the ability will lay fallow. In other words, the disposition to seek out and be open to other viewpoints is what calls the ability into play. Therefore, when teaching thinking, it is not enough to emphasize the development of particular thinking skills and abilities, as many current thinking skills approaches do. Students often fail to put into practice the knowledge and skills they have learned. The best approach combines the development of abilities along with the cultivation of dispositions. (In this connection, see also chapters 12 and 13 on teaching for transfer.)

2. Teaching thinking dispositions will make students more aware of their own thinking patterns. Students are often unaware of their own thinking habits. Poor thinking habits, such as mindlessness or laziness, will override any specific thinking skills that are taught. Therefore, students need to become more aware of their existing thinking patterns at the same time they learn new ones. The teaching of dispositions calls for explicit discussion and examination of students' thinking habits and encourages them to be watchful for opportunities for better thinking. Without cultivating awareness, thinking patterns are unlikely to change.

3. Teaching thinking dispositions will give students a better understanding of what good thinking is. When we speak of someone who is a good thinker, we mean that the person displays tendencies to act in thoughtful ways. Good thinking is a mind-set, a collection of attitudes and inclinations with which one approaches thinking. It is important to paint a picture that captures the dispositional mind-set of good thinking for students. Students have misconceptions about good thinkers, often equating good thinking with "being smart." They need to come to understand that good thinking is not a matter of intellect alone.

4. Teaching thinking dispositions will cultivate ongoing habits of good thinking in students. Unlike the teaching of thinking skills which targets specific behaviors, teaching thinking dispositions aims to develop long-term *habits* of good thinking. By definition, dispositions are abiding tendencies that are displayed over time. Ongoing habits of good thinking become internalized tendencies that students will carry with them into future thinking situations. So, if students develop a disposition to be organized in their thinking, they are likely to approach new thinking situations in an organized way. It is precisely this kind of carryover and sustained engagement that we wish to cultivate in students.

THE BOTTOM LINES: INCORPORATING THINKING DISPOSITIONS INTO THE CULTURE OF THE CLASSROOM

The previous discussion paints a broad picture of a classroom culture intended to foster thinking dispositions. Beyond the broad picture, teachers want to be sure to take certain concrete steps to help build a culture of thinking dispositions in the classroom. Here are some "bottom-line" checkpoints teachers can use to gauge their progress toward establishing a classroom culture that cultivates good thinking dispositions.

1. Model thinking dispositions. Exemplify good thinking dispositions for students to observe in an ongoing way. Use historical figures and famous thinkers as examples. Be a good model of thinking dispositions yourself and encourage students to be good models for one another.

2. Explain thinking dispositions, how they benefit thinking, and when they come into play. Discuss with students how dispositions influence thinking and explain how particular dispositions can benefit good thinking. Discuss and encourage students to employ cues for detecting limits in their thinking and to build their sensitivity to opportunities for better thinking.

3. Encourage interaction. Create opportunities and time for students to experiment in their thinking, to be adventurous, inquiring, careful, and probing. When students are doing lessons, responding to questions, working on problems, or talking in class, encourage them to be alert to their own and others' thinking dispositions. Let students prompt one another to develop good thinking dispositions.

4. Give feedback that is supportive of good thinking dispositions. Establish expectations for thinking dispositions by setting explicit standards, discussing the value of good thinking dispositions, and creating cultural norms for thinking within the classroom. When students display good thinking dispositions, recognize and reinforce the desired dispositions. Try to design motivating activities that include inherent payoffs for good thinking (e.g., self-esteem, success, fun). Give positive feedback and suggestions for how to do better, rather than negative feedback, and encourage students to do the same for one another. Aim to establish a safe haven for thinking which allows students to take risks in their thinking.

Chapter 5 offers several classroom examples of cultivating thinking dispositions. The chapter also includes instructional guidelines for educators interested in trying out some of these ideas in their classrooms and tactics for ongoing enculturation.

▶ 5

Thinking Dispositions: Pictures of Practice

Building a culture of thinking dispositions is a multifaceted enterprise. It calls not only for direct attention to the teaching of dispositions within subject matter lessons, but also for shaping the broader classroom environment.

This chapter builds on the ideas put forth in the previous chapter. The examples offered in the following pages are, in some cases, stand-alone lessons and, in other cases, ongoing culture-building activities. Also included in this chapter are step-by-step instructional guidelines for those who wish to explore some of these techniques in the classroom, as well as tactics for building thinking dispositions into the ongoing culture of the classroom.

Here is a preview of the sections that follow:

1. **Voyage of the *Beagle***
   In this activity, students examine the thinking process of a famous person, Charles Darwin, and identify dispositional aspects of his thinking. Students then embark on their own process of inquiry, during which they attempt to incorporate the dispositions into their thinking process.

2. **Building Cultural Norms**
   Creating a surrounding environment that establishes cultural norms, values, and expectations as well as support for thinking dispositions is a crucial part of successful cultivation of dispositions. Drawing on at-

tributes of cultures in general, this example shows how features of a culture of thinking can be created in the classroom.

3. **Thinking Alarms**
   This activity builds sensitivity to thinking opportunities by making students alert to occasions when their thinking is unnecessarily limited and to situations that present opportunities for better thinking.

4. **Modeling Thinking Dispositions**
   Teacher modeling is an important means of exemplifying good thinking dispositions. In this exercise, the teacher repeatedly models the thinking process and students engage in the same thinking activity, greatly assisted at first by the teacher. Over time, the teacher weans students from this aid.

5. **Taking the Plunge: Guidelines for Instruction**
   Two starting points for beginning to teach thinking dispositions, each with step-by-step guidelines.

6. **Continuing On: Making Thinking Dispositions a Permanent Part of the Classroom Culture**
   More tactics for enculturating thinking dispositions through models, explanation, interaction, and feedback.

7. **Troubleshooting: Questions and Answers about Thinking Dispositions**
   Some common concerns about thinking dispositions.

VOYAGE OF THE *BEAGLE*

Victor Tonnelli had been teaching his unit on Darwin to his eighth-grade science class for years. This time, he decided to begin his unit in a different way. After reading several books on Darwin, he had become intrigued by the process through which Darwin arrived at the theory of evolution. He wanted to share Darwin's creative thinking process with his students and to engage them in some thinking of their own. Mr. Tonnelli walked in the next day with the following passage for his students to read:

> *Charles Darwin's discovery of the principle of natural selection did not happen overnight. The thinking that led to his theory took 15 months to develop. During his five-year voyage on the ship,* The Beagle, *Darwin made detailed observations of animals and organisms on islands off the coast of South America. Darwin raised numerous questions based on his findings: Why did certain species on an island resemble species on the mainland yet always differ in some characteristics? Why was there a gradual change in each species as he traveled down the coast?*

Although he suspected that species develop through evolution, he would not publish his ideas until he could offer an explanation of how evolution occurred. Over the course of 15 months, Darwin generated a number of early theories, each of which he rejected along the way. He was very critical of each proposed theory, being careful to make sure it explained every aspect of what he observed. When he rejected a proposed theory, he worked at forming a new explanation. To refrain from becoming fixed on a single point of view, he explored many alternative interpretations and explanations. . . .

Rather than teaching them about Darwin's conclusion, Mr. Tonnelli embarked on a discussion with his students about Darwin's thinking. "Do you think Darwin's thinking was good?" he asked. The students nodded. "What was good about his thinking?" the teacher queried.

The students ventured some opinions: "it took him a long time, but he didn't give up," "he asked lots of questions," "he came up with lots of ideas, until he got one he thought was right; he didn't just stick to one idea," "he waited until he was sure before he published it." The discussion went on for some time. While the students generated ideas, Mr. Tonnelli wrote them on the blackboard in a more generalized form. The list included the following items:

Features of Thinking

Don't give up
Ask lots of questions
Generate multiple ideas and explanations
Be critical
Don't stop too soon

Next, Mr. Tonnelli wanted to put his students' thinking to the test. He passed out sheets containing some of Darwin's original data, such as the number and characteristics of several species found on various island and mainland locations along the South American coast. The students worked in small groups.

"Now," he said to his students, "I want all of you to pretend you are Darwin taking the five-year voyage on the *Beagle*. In front of you is the most recent data you have collected. I want you to pose some questions that you find interesting and pursue them. Try to come up with what you think is a sensible explanation regarding your question. Feel free to try out any ideas and directions you want even if they seem like long shots. Any explanation is acceptable as long as you can provide reasons to justify it. And this is most important: While you are thinking, I want you to refer to the list on the board frequently to check that you are doing these things in your thinking. Don't forget to use these reminders to check your thinking."

As the students pursued their inquiry, Mr. Tonnelli roamed around the room and listened in on their progress. Whenever he noticed that students were indeed monitoring their thinking and using the reminders to prompt themselves to generate more options or be critical, he was pleased and he told them so. When students were not using the reminders, he reiterated the importance of watching their own thinking and using the reminders.

Meeting the Bottom Lines

How well does this example meet the bottom lines outlined in the previous chapter?

Bottom Line: Model thinking dispositions. yes ■ no □

In this case, a famous historical person, Charles Darwin, serves as a model for thinking dispositions. Students examine his thinking process to learn about and identify good thinking dispositions.

Bottom Line: Explain thinking dispositions, how they benefit thinking, and when they come into play. yes ■ no □

Direct discussion of the features of good thinking helps attune students to the role of dispositions and to specific dispositions that contribute to productive thinking. The students practice identifying good thinking dispositions from other people's as well as their own thinking. Having students do their own investigation creates thinking opportunities in which to play out the dispositions.

Bottom Line: Encourage interaction. yes □ no ■

Except in the minimal sense of students working in groups, this activity does not specifically foster students interacting with one another in ways that boost dispositions.

Bottom Line: Give feedback that is supportive of good thinking dispositions. yes ■ no □

The teacher makes a point of giving immediate feedback and reinforcing thinking dispositions displayed by students while they work.

Following Up: Integrating the Lesson into the Classroom Culture

Mr. Tonnelli can continue to highlight thinking dispositions in his classroom in many ways. He plans to find examples of other famous scientists so he can examine their thinking processes with his students. Since he found it very fruitful to have his students think through some original data, he hopes to build that in from time to time. He aims to have the class continue adding to the "features of thinking" list throughout the year. He will use the list as a constant reminder and offer ample feedback and reinforcement to students when they exhibit good thinking.

BUILDING CULTURAL NORMS

While it is good to devote some time for express teaching of dispositions, as the other examples in this section do, it is equally important to create a surrounding culture of thinking that embodies, supports, and reinforces thinking dispositions. The idea of a culturally supportive environment is that you see good thinking all around you because everybody is doing it. This means making changes in the structure of the classroom that allow dispositions to be a pervasive part of the environment. It involves infusing values and norms into the culture and building expectations for good thinking. One teacher worked on building a culture of thinking dispositions as follows.

Ms. Vasquez, a ninth-grade social studies teacher, understood that students often do not use their thinking capacities to their fullest and wanted to start the new school year with a plan to do something about it in her classroom. She was wise enough to know that isolated lessons would not achieve her goal. Instead, she decided to develop a classroom atmosphere that would encourage good thinking among her students. She developed the following ideas for creating a thinking culture that she implemented in her classroom.

Joint Understanding

At the outset, she aimed to establish a joint understanding about the norms for thinking. Following a problem-solving session at the beginning of the year, she challenged her students to evaluate their thinking: "Were you a good thinker or not a good thinker?" When students offered their assessments, Ms. Vasquez had them talk about the pros and cons of their thinking. She then discussed with them the value of some particular thinking dispositions that she introduced. For instance, she asked, "What is good about being organized in your thinking?" The students had no trouble offering good rationales for organized thinking. Similarly, they jointly established the value of other dispositions the teacher mentioned: being curious and questioning, being broad and adventurous, and being clear and careful.

- Challenge students to evaluate their thinking.
- Discuss the pros and cons of particular thinking dispositions.
- Establish joint understanding of the value of thinking dispositions.
- Explicitly set expectations for good thinking.

After establishing a joint understanding of their value, the teacher set up expectations for students to display the dispositions. She said, "Now that we see why this kind of thinking is good, let us try to practice good thinking. Throughout this year, I'm going to be watching to see if you are practicing them—and your classmates will be watching too."

Artifacts

Every culture has artifacts that embody and symbolize the norms and values of the culture. For example, the American flag is an artifact that symbolizes unity built out of many parts. Ms. Vasquez created physical artifacts around her classroom to represent the thinking norms. She hung a large poster on the wall for the entire school year. It read:

THINKING BE'S

- Be curious and questioning
- Be broad and adventurous
- Be clear and careful
- Be organized

Ms. Vasquez frequently had her students refer to the thinking be's poster. Whenever they were solving a problem, doing an assignment, thinking of ideas for a project, taking a test, or completing any other thinking activity, she would remind them to look at the thinking be's list. Soon, the students were reminding each other before the teacher mentioned it.

Ms. Vasquez created other artifacts as well. In the middle of written assignments and tests, between problems, she would stick in a reminder about the thinking be's. When correcting papers, if she noticed that a student missed the opportunity to explore broader options or to be more clear or to exhibit any other thinking disposition, she would write a reminder right on the corrected paper.

- Create visual artifacts, such as lists or posters, as reminders of thinking dispositions.
- In written assignments, plant reminders to use thinking dispositions.
- Give feedback when correcting papers or written work.

Constructive Evaluation

Part of a culture consists of upholding cultural expectations and establishing adherence to those standards by members of the community. Ms. Vasquez, therefore, encouraged students to evaluate each other's thinking as well as her own thinking in an ongoing way. After a student presented a report or solved a problem, she would ask the other students, "What were the best parts of Kathy's thinking?" Then, "Kathy, where do you think you could do better?" And then, "Perhaps some of the rest of you can offer another thinking tip?" At the end of class discussion, she might pose the question, "Was our thinking as a group good thinking?" She even subjected her own thinking to the test: "What did you like about the way I made that decision? And how can I make such decisions better in the future?"

At first students were reluctant to critique each other's thinking, but after a while they became used to it. Ms. Vasquez made sure that the evaluating was done in a supportive way by always calling for positive points and then suggestions for doing better. Ms. Vasquez often had her students work in collaborative groups, and she en-

- Have students evaluate one another's thinking in a supportive way.
- Encourage students to be constructive, not critical.
- Structure cooperative learning situations; encourage students to learn from each other and provide mutual support.

couraged them to give themselves feedback as groups about their thinking and learning processes. Soon, playing mutual watchdog evolved into a good-humored game. Ms. Vasquez was very pleased to see that the students could be watchful in a constructive way.

Meeting the Bottom Lines

The aim of Ms. Vasquez was to establish cultural norms for good thinking dispositions in her classroom. How thoroughly did she use the bottom lines to do so?

Bottom Line: Model thinking dispositions. yes ■ no ☐

While the introductory lesson included no explicit modeling, later on Ms. Vasquez encouraged the students to become models for one another, as well as being a model herself.

Bottom Line: Explain thinking dispositions, how they benefit thinking, and when they come into play. yes ■ no ☐

In introducing thinking dispositions, Ms. Vasquez engaged the students in explicit discussions of thinking dispositions. Throughout the year, opportunistic reminders to pay attention to the dispositions on the thinking be's poster provided occasions for further explanation.

Bottom Line: Encourage interaction. yes ■ no ☐

Interaction is the centerpiece of this activity because that is what building cultural understanding is all about. At the outset, having students work together to build norms, establish expectations, and offer mutual support and feedback was crucial for creating a culture. Ms. Vasquez continued her emphasis on students' interaction with her and one another throughout the year.

Bottom Line: Give feedback that is supportive of good thinking dispositions. yes ■ no ☐

Ms. Vasquez deliberately sought out occasions to provide feedback and encouraged students to offer feedback to one another.

THINKING ALARMS

We all like to believe that we are good thinkers. So it is not always easy to see when we are not thinking our best. However, a key aspect of building good thinking dispositions is noticing when we fall short of our thinking capabilities. Many people let lazy or disorganized thinking slip by, thereby missing opportunities for better thinking. To cultivate ongoing thinking dispositions in students, we want to build their *sensitivity* to thinking challenges. Sensitivity means that students can detect limits in their thinking and occasions when they could push their thinking further.

One classroom technique for encouraging students to monitor their own thinking is the "thinking alarm." A thinking alarm is a signal that alerts you to an occasion when your thinking might miss something. It tells you that you need to kick in one of the dispositions for good thinking. For example, hasty thinking is a signal that you are not giving enough time for thinking. Below are some thinking alarms and the corresponding dispositions that can help improve thinking.

Thinking Alarm	Thinking Disposition
Lazy thinking	Be curious andquestioning
Narrow thinking	Be broad and adventurous
Messy thinking	Be clear and careful
Scattered thinking	Be organized
Hasty thinking	Give thinking time

Here is how one teacher introduces the thinking alarm to his students. This lesson is about identifying narrow thinking. He starts by presenting a problem to the students.

Teacher: Imagine that you are the principal of this school and all the janitors decide to go on strike because they think they are not getting enough pay. What would you do?

Student #1: I would fire them all.

Student #2: Maybe I would fire the ones who weren't doing a good job, but keep the ones who were doing a good job.

Student #3: I would see if there was any money to pay them more, but if there wasn't, they would have to take the same pay or lose their jobs.

Teacher: What do you think is similar about all the responses? *(The students remain silent.)* All of these solutions seem to be about whether or not the janitors would be fired or lose their jobs. Are these the only kinds of solutions possible? *(The students shake their heads.)* "Now let's stand back, as we often do, and evaluate our thinking. How was our thinking?"

Student #3: Not so good because we didn't come up with enough different kinds of answers.

Teacher: Ah, then. This should set off an alarm in our heads, we might call it a *thinking alarm*. In this case, the thinking alarm tells us that our thinking was too narrow, we did not think about it from enough different angles. *(He writes the following on a wall chart)*

!!! Thinking Alarm !!!

Narrow thinking

Teacher: Thinking alarms are signals that we want to be alert to at all times in our thinking. Whenever you detect the signs of a thinking alarm in the course of your thinking, an alarm should go off in your head. So, for this particular thinking alarm, whenever you see yourself proposing ideas that are very similar, the alarm should go off alerting you to the possibility of narrow thinking.

But what do you do after you have noticed a thinking alarm? You need something to tell yourself about what to do. So, a "tell myself" is a reminder to yourself about what you can do when you have hit a thinking alarm. In this case, you might tell yourself to be broad and adventurous, to look for alternative approaches and solutions. It means being flexible and looking for different angles of approach. *He writes again:*

!!! Thinking Alarm !!!

Narrow thinking

Tell Myself

Be broad and adventurous
Look for alternatives
Be flexible

The teacher asks his students to use the tell myself reminders to combat narrow thinking. The students come up with more varied solutions to the janitor problem, such as negotiating with the janitors, waiting out the strike to see if the janitors give in, assessing the possibility of getting replacement workers. The students continue to devise more inventive and elaborate solutions.

Over time, the class begins to enjoy the game of looking for a thinking alarm during each others' thinking or the class's collective thinking. The teacher encourages class monitoring of each others' thinking in a supportive rather than judgmental way. Thus, it becomes part of the culture to watch for opportunities to improve thinking.

Meeting the Bottom Lines

Thinking alarms are ways of building students' sensitivity to recognizing thinking opportunities on their own. How does this introduction of thinking alarms into the culture of the classroom draw on the four cultural forces?

Bottom Line: Model thinking dispositions. yes ☐ no ■

Direct modeling does not play a significant role in this example.

Bottom Line: Explain thinking dispositions, how they benefit thinking, and when they come into play. yes ■ no ☐

The teacher explains the concept of thinking alarms and tell myselfs at the outset, providing a framework with which the students can work for the rest of the year. Thinking alarms build students' sensitivity to thinking opportunities by teaching cues that signal occasions for engaging thinking dispositions.

Bottom Line: Encourage interaction. yes ■ no ☐

The teacher interacts with his students to draw their attention to thinking alarms and tell myselfs.

Bottom Line: Give feedback that is supportive of good thinking dispositions. yes ■ no ☐

The teacher encourages the students to give themselves feedback on their thinking—this is what leads to the thinking alarms and tell myselfs. Students give each other feedback by helping one another watch for opportunities to improve their thinking.

Following Up: Integrating the Lesson into the Classroom Culture

The teacher in this example follows through on the thinking alarm theme by planning to feature one thinking alarm and its associated disposition per month. Perhaps one month he focuses on the disposition to give thinking time. At the beginning of the month, he presents a lesson like the one included here that explains the importance of giving thinking time. Then throughout the month, when students are doing regular class work, he often reminds them to watch out for being too hasty and to slow down to allow time for thinking.

MODELING THINKING DISPOSITIONS

How can we get students involved in the spirit of scientific thinking and investigation at a young age? Any elementary school teacher could tell you that children surely have a lot of curiosity about the natural world, but it seldom goes beyond the initial questions. What can be done to help them become more inclined to probe deeper and sustain longer lines of thinking and inquiry?

One answer lies in the modeling of thinking dispositions by adults. If we want students to learn good thinking dispositions, we have to model them ourselves. The researchers Ann Marie Palincsar and Ann Brown introduced a very effective modeling technique for teaching reading comprehension, called Reciprocal Teaching (Palincsar & Brown, 1984). After reading a paragraph together, the teacher initially models the process (forming a question about the paragraph, constructing a summary, clarifying, making predictions), eventually turning it over to the students. When students first undertake the process, the teacher coaches them extensively. Then, as students become more proficient, the teacher turns more of the task over to them. At different times, the teacher and students take turns playing the role of the teacher (the one who works through the process); hence, the term Reciprocal Teaching.

Although Reciprocal Teaching was designed for teaching reading comprehension, the broad technique applies equally well to the teaching of thinking dispositions. Here is an example of how this kind of modeling approach might be used to improve science inquiry in younger students.

Throughout the school year, Madeline Chun periodically brought objects from nature into her fourth-grade class. The first day she brought a starfish and began thinking aloud about it, asking questions and explaining her thought process to the class. In the midst of her inquiry, she occasionally stopped to explain her thinking.

Ms. Chun's Questions	*Ms. Chun's Explanation of Her Thinking*
Why does a starfish have five points? Why not four or six? Is it alive? Why does it seem to be alive in water but not on land? What does it eat? How does it eat? Who are its predators? How does it move?	I often start by *asking lots of questions,* whatever comes to mind, just to get started.
What if you moved it to a place where it had no predators?	I try to *be imaginative and adventurous* in my questions. I want to discover interesting things.

Ms. Chun's Questions	*Ms. Chun's Explanation of Her Thinking*
Would the starfish population keep growing and growing? What if I cut off one of its points? Would it grow back?	Then, I will *focus in on a question* I want to investigate further. I don't want to just brainstorm, but to get somewhere.
The question I want to investigate further is: Is the starfish alive?	
First I will consider what I know about things that are alive: they eat, reproduce, many breathe, some but not all can move. I can use these ideas to be organized about how I investigate whether or not the starfish is alive. (Ms. Chun continues on with further questions along these lines.)	I want to *be organized* about how I proceed at investigating my question, so I can really settle some questions.

For the next lesson, Ms. Chun brought in a piece of lava. She told the students what it was and invited them to conduct the investigation. She assisted and coached them whenever they needed help.

Student #1: I don't know what to ask. It looks like a rock. Is it a rock?

Ms. Chun: Remember to start by brainstorming. Ask lots of questions, whatever comes to mind.

Student #2: Well, it has holes. How did the holes get there?

Student #1: If it has holes, does that mean it will sink if you put it in water?

Student #3: I've heard that lava comes from volcanoes. Does it have anything to do with when the volcano blows up?

Ms. Chun: That's good. Now try for some more imaginative and adventurous questions.

Student #4: What if this isn't from a volcano on earth, but is from another planet?

Student #2: I wonder if lava is good for anything. Can you use it for anything?

Ms. Chun: Great! Now spin those thoughts out. What other questions do these questions suggest?

Student #4: Well, how would it get here? Maybe it's a meteor. Are there really volcanoes on other planets?

Student #2: It's really light. Maybe you could build buildings out of it. I wonder how strong it is? Is it strong enough?

Ms. Chun: Wonderful! To keep going with those ideas, you might ask some questions about what kind of proof you would need. Try that.

Thereafter, each time she brought an item for investigation, Ms. Chun offered a little less coaching, allowing the students to get used to doing it on their own. She made a point of encouraging students when they exhibited good thinking dispositions. The investigator role rotated among the teacher and students, so occasionally the teacher would have more opportunities to model and reinforce the process. Ms. Chun asked the students to coach one another. Pretty soon, the students were able to generate and focus questions quite well on their own.

Meeting the Bottom Lines

Modeling good thinking dispositions is especially important when working with younger children, because witnessing and emulating dispositions early on makes a difference for long-term thinking habits. This example couples teacher modeling with feedback.

Bottom Line: Model thinking dispositions. yes ■ no ☐

Ms. Chun started out modeling good thinking by explaining her thought process aloud. Eventually, she faded out her direct modeling and turned the thinking process over to the students.

Bottom Line: Explain thinking dispositions, how they benefit thinking, and when they come into play. yes ■ no ☐

As Ms. Chun modeled, she also explained what she was doing and why.

Bottom Line: Encourage interaction. yes ■ no ☐

Reciprocal Teaching relies on interaction. In this case, while one person was going through the thinking process, others observed and took turns in the coaching role.

Bottom Line: Ensure feedback and create expectations for good thinking dispositions. yes ■ no ☐

Feedback is critical to this kind of modeling. An important feature of Ms. Chun's approach was that coaching and feedback were given and received by everyone.

Following Up: Integrating the Lesson into the Classroom Culture

Ms. Chun continues to model thinking dispositions and provide informative feedback. The rotating format allows her to periodically model thinking dispositions to reinforce the behaviors, then turn it back to the students. She constantly brings in new items for investigation so that question asking becomes a regular thinking challenge.

TAKING THE PLUNGE: GUIDELINES FOR INSTRUCTION

If the techniques described in the above examples intrigue you, you may be interested in trying them out in your own classroom. Perhaps you have a clear notion of how best to get started in your setting, in which case by all means follow your plan. If you'd like some ideas, here are a couple of "plunge points"—starting points for instruction. Take a look at both of them, see which one suits you, and simply follow the instructions step by step.

Plunge Point #1

1. Reread the example "Voyage of the *Beagle*" from the beginning of this chapter and use it as a guide to design your own lesson.

2. Choose an example of thinking, decision making, problem solving, or investigation done by yourself or by famous figures appropriate to your subject area where students can analyze the thinking. Using the example as an entry point, begin discussing the notion of thinking dispositions with students as Mr. Tonnelli did.

3. Have students decide what characteristics they believe are key to good thinking. Record the characteristics they choose and put a version of it up as a poster, so that the written list becomes a jointly shared, physical artifact of the culture.

4. Engage students in their own thinking challenges, such as investigation or decision making. Ask them to make a point of using the thinking dispositions on the list while they are doing their thinking.

5. Identify several points in the next few weeks where students will be doing independent thinking. Remind them of the list of thinking dispositions and remind them to use the dispositions while doing their thinking.

6. **Reflect.** After taking any of the above plunges, you are likely to have a more concrete sense of what focusing on thinking dispositions in the classroom is all about. So, at that point, it is useful to reflect on your progress.

- Review how your conception of thinking dispositions has gradually changed over the past few weeks. Ask yourself, what were the classroom or planning events that really made the concept become clearer for you?
- Ask yourself what seem to be students' strengths and weaknesses in grasping and adopting thinking dispositions. Which concepts do they understand? Which ones do they have difficulty with, why, and what might you do about it?

Plunge Point #2

1. Make your own list of dispositions that you think contribute to good thinking. Reflect on what works and does not work well in your own thinking. Assess your students' thinking. Where do they perform well and what habits interfere with their thinking? Remember that some dispositions can work against good thinking rather than for it—the disposition to reach hasty conclusions, for instance. Keep these troublesome dispositions in mind when talking with your students.

2. Discuss in class the concept of dispositions and how they can influence thinking. Describe some target dispositions for good thinking. Let students examine dispositions in other areas of their lives and discuss how they would try to improve them. For example, how could they try to improve a disposition to procrastinate or to be argumentative? Ask students what could be done in class to help everyone improve his or her thinking dispositions. Let the class reach agreement among themselves on how to go about fostering their own good thinking dispositions, then ask them to make a plan to do so.

CONTINUING ON: MAKING THINKING DISPOSITIONS A PERMANENT PART OF THE CLASSROOM CULTURE

Once you have taken the plunge, either by following one of the above suggestions or by experimenting on your own, how can you make thinking dispositions a permanent and pervasive part of the classroom culture?

A useful guideline is to aim for a combination of specific lessons and instructional moments tucked into other kinds of lessons, all the while taking advantage of the four cultural forces—models, explanation, interaction, and feedback. The following are suggestions in each of these areas. Some suggestions involve the design of specific, focused lessons, while others are geared toward creating an ongoing culture of thinking.

Models of Thinking Dispositions

- Design specific lessons around people who model the desired thinking dispositions, similar to the "Voyage of the *Beagle*" or the "Modeling" examples in this chapter.
- Center lessons on discussion of a physical artifact, such as a poster listing thinking dispositions.
- In the course of everyday practice, try to model good thinking dispositions in your own discourse.
- Have artifacts around all the time as reminders to students, in the form of posters, reminders on written assignments, reminders in your written feedback to students on assignments (see the artifacts section in "Building Cultural Norms").

Explanations of Thinking Dispositions

- Plan focused lessons around specific thinking dispositions, using the sample lessons "Voyage of the *Beagle*," "Thinking Alarms," and "Modeling" as guides.
- Look for "on-the-fly" opportunities in the middle of your regular subject matter teaching to remind students about key thinking dispositions.
- Try to build students' sensitivity to thinking challenges and opportunities. Use explicit techniques such as thinking alarms or more informal reminders to help students become aware of their own thinking dispositions and to detect cues for opportunities to employ good thinking.

Interactions with Thinking Dispositions

- Create thinking opportunities. Be sure to make time for students to tackle extended thinking challenges and put good thinking dispositions into practice.
- Design thinking dispositions lessons that explore new patterns of teacher/student interaction, such as the reciprocal teaching method discussed in the "Modeling Thinking Dispositions" section.
- Allow ample occasion during lessons for students to interact with one another in ways that can reinforce displays of good thinking dispositions.
- Develop cultural habits and understandings that are an integral part of everyday classroom practice. Build joint understandings and expectations about good thinking dispositions as a group through periodic discussion and repeated acknowledgment of the understandings, as described in the "Building Cultural Norms" section.

Feedback on Thinking Dispositions

- Give consistent feedback that encourages students when they display good thinking dispositions. Provide feedback for students' work in class as well as for written assignments.

- Cultivate a habit among students of assessing their own and each other's thinking as described in the "Building Cultural Norms" section.

Checking Your Progress

A good check on your progress in enculturating dispositions is to review your teaching activities related to dispositions at the end of every week. Using a weekly chart that you complete at the week's end, you can see how well you are covering the four modes of enculturation: models, explanation, interaction, and feedback. Table 5.1 is a sample chart filled out with some possible thinking activities a teacher might have done during the week.

TROUBLESHOOTING: QUESTIONS AND ANSWERS ABOUT THINKING DISPOSITIONS

It seems that dispositions are like personality traits and may be hard to change. Can thinking dispositions really be cultivated?

Thinking dispositions, like other dispositions, can definitely be cultivated. Consider how children growing up in a family often pick up dispositions from the family culture, or how children that associate with a certain group pick up dispositions from the group. Naturally, since dispositions tend to be fairly stable, dispositional change comes slower than other types of learning. When teaching thinking dispositions, therefore, it is important to recognize that you are after long-term change and that you cannot expect immediate outcomes.

From my experience, I see that students already have dispositions that affect thinking. Unfortunately, many of their natural dispositions work against good thinking. How can I deal with students' existing dispositions?

The first step is to recognize that students are not blank slates when it comes to thinking dispositions. Students do have existing dispositions that affect thinking in strong and entrenched ways. Some of these, such as mindlessness or unwillingness to exert thinking effort, work against good thinking. Many of the thinking dispositions we would like to see—open-mindedness, for instance—run contrary to the natural tendency of the mind. People are disposed to be rather closed-minded because of a number of cognitive and affective factors. So it is inevitable that you will be working against some preexisting tendencies.

One way to combat existing dispositions is to get students' thinking dispositions, positive and negative, out on the table. Explicit discussion of and reflection on their own dispositions will help students take stock of their

TABLE 5.1 Thinking Dispositions Weekly Progress Chart

	MONDAY	TUESDAY	WEDNESDAY	THURSDAY	FRIDAY
Models		I modeled broad, adventurous, flexible thinking through an example.			
Explanation	Introduced a lesson on thinking alarms (featuring narrow thinking) and thinking alarms poster.	Practiced looking for cases of narrow thinking; discussed disposition to be broad, adventurous.	I explained the concept of narrow thinking, added it to the thinking alarm poster.		Added another thinking alarm: scattered thinking.
Interaction	Interacted with students using thinking alarms.		During a debate, I had students watch for narrow thinking in each other's arguments.	I had students collaborate on short essays as they paid attention to the thinking alarms.	Discussed scattered thinking with students.
Feedback	Had students give themselves feedback to identify thinking alarms.		I gave positive feedback when students showed they detected narrow thinking.	While reading the written essays, I made positive comments whenever students showed that they were thinking more broadly.	

thinking. Rather than expecting students to adopt a new disposition whole-heartedly right away, it is helpful to first begin by getting students to experience the feeling of doing things in a way that is opposite their natural tendency. Then you can discuss the differences with them.

Recognize that it may be too much to expect students to adopt the whole attitude and spirit of a disposition immediately. Instead, you may want to foster just the habit of behaving in the desired way. If you simultaneously model the spirit, give reasons for the disposition, and establish cultural values and expectations, the attitude and affect may follow later once the behavioral habit has developed. Creating a social context that fosters thinking dispositions is extremely important in combating negative dispositions because it provides an environment that both expects and supports good thinking.

I am used to teaching concrete content knowledge and skills. Thinking dispositions are hard to get a handle on. I don't know how to teach anything so amorphous. How can I work it into my regular curriculum?

Indeed, thinking dispositions are subtle and often difficult to see. Yet, you probably already implicitly foster certain aspects of thinking by the way you reward certain kinds of student responses and by the thinking you yourself display. The teaching of thinking dispositions does not require separate attention away from your regular teaching. You can attend to thinking dispositions whenever thinking opportunities arise in the course of teaching the subject area. The aim is to improve students' thinking dispositions in real and pertinent thinking situations so that they carry them over to future thinking challenges.

▶ 6

Mental Management

*Mental Management: 1. The art of reflecting on and
guiding one's own thinking processes. 2. Metacognition.*

The psychologist Ellen Langer tells the story of a woman who, when cooking a roast, always cut off a little slice before putting it in the pot. When asked why she did this, the woman confessed that she didn't know—she was simply following a family tradition and cooking the roast the way her mother did. However, the query aroused the woman's curiosity, and she went to her mother and asked her the reason for cutting off the slice. Her mother gave the same explanation: she did it because *her* mother did. Finally, the woman asked her grandmother the reason for cutting off the slice. "Because that was the only way it would fit in the pot," her grandmother replied (Langer, 1989).

Langer's point is that all too often we mindlessly follow routines and fail to reflect on the effectiveness of our thinking. Her point is a good one: While no one wants to be intensively self-critical all of the time, the ability to watch and critique one's own thinking is a key aspect of human intelligence.

The novelist and philosopher Albert Camus once observed that a good thinker is a person whose mind watches itself. In recent years, many educators and psychologists have made a similar claim. They argue that, to a considerable extent, the good thinker in virtually any field is intellectually self-watchful, self-guiding, and self-assessing.

Intellectual self-watchfulness is a learned ability, and learning to be good at it has much in common with learning to be a good manager. Good managers in any setting share a similar craft—they tend to be astute observers, careful evaluators, and effective leaders. These same abilities are present in good *mental* managers. They are people who can manage their own thought processes effectively—people who can step back from their own thinking and watch it as it is happening, diagnosing shortcomings and assessing strengths.

Surprisingly, although mental management is to a large extent a learned ability, it is rarely directly taught in school. Perhaps this is because traditional schooling tends to focus children's attention exclusively on thinking products outside the self—on texts, facts, and the "right answers"—and rarely provides learners with opportunities to reflect on their own inner thinking processes. But neglecting to teach mental management does a disservice to students: research shows that students who have opportunities to develop their metacognitive abilities tend to perform better in many learning situations (Pressley, Borkowski, & Schneider, 1987).

How do you teach students how to be good mental managers? Here is an example. Ms. Orman is a fifth-grade teacher who has been trying to cultivate her students' mental management skills. She worries that students depend too much on grades and other external evaluations to tell them whether they are thinking well. Grades are important, Ms. Orman admits, but her students won't be in school forever, and she wants them to become more *self*-evaluative about thinking. She wants them to practice standing back and deciding for themselves when their thinking is going well or not so well, and deciding for themselves how to guide themselves towards better thinking practices.

To achieve her goal, Ms. Orman has been giving her students plenty of time to consciously stand back and reflect on their own thinking. Here is a discussion she conducted with her fifth graders, immediately following a math quiz.

Ms. Orman: Now that the quiz is over, let's stand back and think about the thinking we've just done. Close your eyes for a moment and review how your mind has been working. Ask yourself: "What parts of my thinking went well?" "What parts of my thinking didn't go so well?" Take a minute to reflect. I'll let you know when the minute is up. (*Ms. Orman makes sure to give students a stretch of quiet time for reflection, before she asks them to speak.*) O.K., what are your thoughts?

Student #1: My thinking went well in the beginning, because it was long division, and I know how to do that pretty well. But then I forgot to look at the time. I had to rush through the last section, and I didn't have time to check my work.

Ms. Orman: That's an interesting observation. Any ideas about how you could make your thinking better?

Student #1: I guess I could try to remind myself to check the time more often. So I won't have to rush at the end.

Ms. Orman: Good idea. I'll remind you of your idea next time we take a quiz. Does anyone have any other thought about his thinking?

Student #2: I do. My thinking didn't go well when I came to the part with word problems. Especially that problem about the trains going past each other in two different directions. My problem is that I think too hard in just one way. Like with the trains. I thought that you had to do the problem by using multiplication. So I kept trying to come up with the right numbers to multiply. But I finally realized—after I had wasted tons of time!—that you had to think about it completely differently, as a division problem, with fractions.

Ms. Orman: So you're saying that one way your thinking didn't go so well is that you tried too hard in just one way. I can understand that. It is a problem I sometimes have with thinking, too. I believe it's a very common problem. Put your mental manager hat on: do you have any ideas about what you could do to avoid it?

Student #2: Hmm . . . I guess I could try to watch my thinking more carefully, and remind myself that when I feel myself thinking really hard, I should ask myself whether I should be trying to look for other ways to think.

Ms. Orman: Good idea! I think I'll try it myself.

WHAT IS MENTAL MANAGEMENT?

Ms. Orman believes that learning to be a good thinker involves learning to be an effective and creative mental manager. So she provides students with lots of opportunities to reflect on their own thinking, and—very importantly—she encourages them to take an active role in evaluating their own thinking and inventing better ways to manage it.

Mental management is the activity of reflecting on and evaluating one's own thinking processes. Sometimes called *metacognition*, it is a key component of good thinking, and a phenomenon that has received quite a bit of attention in contemporary cognitive psychology.

Consider this striking feature of human cognition: We can *think about our own thinking*. Not only can we engage in high-level cognitive activities like making decisions, solving problems, and making plans, we can also stand back and oversee our thinking as we do these things. We can watch our own thinking *as it happens* and decide how to direct it. For example, while trying to solve a problem, we can note that our thinking is stuck on one track and decide to take a more creative approach. Similarly, we can decide we ought to be more careful about plans we're making, or more thoughtful about a decision we're considering. This dimension of cognition—the ability to reflect on and evaluate the flow of thought—is the mental management, or metacognitive, dimension of thinking. It is essential to good thinking because of its regulative and evaluative role. In this chapter, we show how explicit attention to metacognition can be woven into regular instruction.

Three Thinking Pitfalls

When should students practice good mental management? Almost anytime. But here are three opportunities in the course of student learning that are particularly key. The first is *before* a thinking challenge; the second is *during* a thinking challenge; the third is *after* a thinking challenge. A thinking challenge is any complex or nonroutine thinking task. The challenge might be studying for a test, conducting an experiment, researching a topic, making a decision, writing an essay, making a plan, taking a quiz, working in a group, making a painting, listening to a lecture, or watching a film. In Chapter 7, we describe FourThought—a step-by-step mental management strategy that guides students through the "before," "during," and "after" opportunities of virtually any thinking challenge. But before going into detail about this strategy, it is worth taking a closer look at the typical pitfalls in thinking at each of these three thinking junctures—pitfalls that are counterproductive, that block good thinking, and that can be avoided through thoughtful and strategic mental management.

The **"before thinking"** pitfall occurs when people plunge into a thinking challenge without adequate mental preparation—without taking the time to clear their minds, to focus their thoughts, and to visualize what's upcoming. This pitfall can cause hasty and unfocused thinking. Good mental managers are aware of this and take steps to mentally prepare themselves before a thinking challenge.

The **"during thinking"** pitfall occurs when people proceed through a thinking challenge without taking account of the larger picture—without taking the time to set goals and standards, and without making the effort to stand back and monitor how their thinking is going. This pitfall leads to an array of problems, including narrow thinking, one-dimensional thinking, and unimaginative thinking. Good mental managers take steps to avoid this pitfall. They make a point of identifying their goals and standards, and they stay on the lookout for promising new directions in which to guide the flow of their thoughts.

The **"after thinking"** pitfall occurs when, at the close of a thinking challenge, people neglect to take time to reflect on how thinking went. Partially, this occurs because of a lack of opportunity. In the ever faster-paced school curriculum, the rush for coverage overtakes us, and we are rarely able to provide the time for students to conscientiously reflect on work they have just completed. But even if time for reflection *is* available, the habit of reflection is by and large a learned habit, and the rush for coverage is only one instance of a larger human pitfall. We're almost *always* in a hurry, and in humankind's rush to get on with life, the reflective temperament must be cultivated. To avoid the "after thinking" pitfall, reflective mental managers make a conscious effort to run their minds back over the highs and lows of the thinking challenge they just finished. They reevaluate the appropriateness of their goals and standards, and thoughtfully reflect on ways to improve their thinking in the future.

WHY IS MENTAL MANAGEMENT IMPORTANT?

All this may sound good in theory, but what concrete advantages do students gain by learning mental management techniques? In what ways will students' thinking noticeably develop? Four important ways stand out:

1. Mental management cultivates cognitive resourcefulness. When faced with a problem or difficulty in thinking, the good mental manager stands back and asks, "What can I think of to do here?" rather than just unreflectively falling into something and doing it. For example, FourThought, a mental management strategy we describe in Chapter 7, helps students to resourcefully manage their thinking during complex thinking tasks. It directs them to stay on the lookout for troublesome thinking junctures and helps them to seek solutions and alternative approaches *on their own*. Mental management techniques like this one teach students how to tackle thinking challenges independently and creatively, rather than passively waiting to be told what to do.

2. Mental management promotes responsible and independent thinking. We aim to educate children to become thoughtful, responsible members of society. An important part of being a thoughtful adult is the ability to set one's own goals and standards, rather than mindlessly following in others' footsteps. It takes strength of character to establish and achieve one's own goals and standards. But it also takes thoughtful practice to develop skill in setting reasonable goals and standards against the backdrop of one's capacities and tendencies. The thoughtful practice of mental management, even in the early grades, gives students the tools they need to develop into responsible, independent-thinking adults.

3. Mental management fosters strategic thinking and planfulness. A fundamental mental management tactic is to momentarily step back from the flow of one's thinking and consider how to proceed. More often than not, deciding how to proceed involves planning or strategizing. For instance, suppose you have an important decision to make. As a good mental manager you want to avoid making a hasty decision, so you plan steps to take to make sure you think through your decision carefully. Maybe you decide to use a full-fledged decision-making strategy you know about, to help you work through the entire decision. Or maybe your goal is to conduct a broad search for options, so you use a strategy such as webbing or brainstorming to help you look for lots of creative ideas. As educators know all too well, students are not automatically planful and strategic. It takes a special mental effort for students to think ahead and strategically plan how to tackle a thinking challenge. Practicing mental management teaches students how and when to make this move.

4. Mental management is a learnable aspect of intelligence. Some psychologists maintain that metacognition—what we are calling "mental management"—is a hallmark of human consciousness: A mind that can make its own thoughts an object of thought is a distinctly human mind. Not surprisingly, most theories of intelligence identify metacognition as key: For example, Binet, the father of intelligence theory, pointed to "autocriticism"—the ability to reflect on and regulate cognition—as a central component of intelligence (Binet & Simon, 1905). More recently, cognitive theorists of intelligence such as Robert Sternberg, and David Perkins, among others have stressed the key role of mental self-government, and self-regulation in intelligence (Sternberg, 1985; Perkins, in press).

In plain language, what such research on intelligence shows is this: How intelligently you think and act has a lot to do with how well you are able to monitor and reflect on your own thinking. But while the *capacity* for mental management may be innate in humans (as is, for example, the capacity to learn a language), the good news is that metacognitive *ability* can be increased: We can learn how to become more aware of our own thinking processes, and learn how to assess and guide them more productively. Insofar as mental management is teachable (and we hope this chapter convinces you that it is), intelligence is learnable.

THE BOTTOM LINES: INCORPORATING MENTAL MANAGEMENT INTO THE CULTURE OF THE CLASSROOM

If mental management is teachable, how can it best be taught? Like the other dimensions of good thinking described in this volume, students' mental management is cultivated most effectively by taking advantage of the four cultural forces in the classroom: models, explanations, interaction, and feedback. In bottom line language, this suggests that educators should:

1. Model mental management. Make sure to model mental management when teaching. Show students how you yourself reflect on your own thinking, and how you guide yourself to be a better thinker. Also draw students' attention to examples of others who think about their thinking: artists, scientists, musicians, writers, fellow students, and teachers.

2. Explain key mental management concepts and practices. Straightforwardly explain to students the purpose of mental management and provide direct instruction in its strategies and techniques.

3. Organize opportunities for student/student and teacher/student interactions around mental management. Through discussions and group work, make sure students have the opportunity to talk with one another about their thinking as individuals and their thinking in groups, and to work together on becoming better mental managers.

4. Be sure that students get feedback about their mental management practices. Show that mental management is valued in the classroom: Critique and encourage students' mental management as it is happening, and arrange opportunities for students to give each other feedback about their mental management practices.

Chapter 7 provides classroom examples of mental management in practice, and a description of a powerful mental management strategy called FourThought, for use in virtually any context and at any grade level. Also included in the following chapter are instructional guidelines for those wishing to experiment with mental management in their classrooms and suggestions for how to use the four cultural forces to keep the spirit of mental management alive.

▶ 7

Mental Management: Pictures of Practice

What does it look like to teach mental management? This chapter offers three vignettes that illustrate different instructional approaches, along with advice about how to start teaching mental management yourself. Here is an overview of the sections to come.

1. **"Put on Your Thinking Cap"—A New Meaning**
   Getting to know your thinking self and inventing ways to make thinking better can be fun. This example shows how one teacher guides her young students in an exploration of themselves as thinkers.

2. **FourThought: A Mental Management Strategy**
   This extra long section (really four examples in one) describes a versatile four-step strategy that helps students avoid thinking defaults and provides sound mental management guidance for virtually any thinking challenge.

3. **Modeling Mental Management: An Example in Real Time**
   There is no such thing as a perfect human thinker who never experiences any obstacles to good thinking. This is an example of how one teacher models the thinking processes behind good mental management in a way that underscores the real challenges and obstacles to good thinking that all thinkers face.

4. **Taking the Plunge: Guidelines for Instruction**
   Two starting points for introducing mental management into the classroom.

5. **Continuing On: Making Mental Management a Permanent Part of the Classroom Culture**
Tactics for keeping mental management a vibrant part of the classroom culture, organized according to the four cultural forces—models, explanation, interaction, and feedback.

6. **Troubleshooting: Questions and Answers about Mental Management**
Common concerns about teaching mental management and what to do about them.

PUT ON YOUR THINKING CAP

Ms. Greenway wants her fourth graders to learn to be better mental managers. She also knows that traditional schooling rarely highlights mental management, and that the idea of thinking about their own thinking will be new and a little strange to her students. So she decides to build an activity around a familiar concept—the idea of a thinking cap. Monday morning she has this to say to her students:

"On Friday of this week, we're going to do an unusual activity. I'm going to ask each one of you to draw your own custom-made thinking cap, an imaginary hat that will make you be the best thinker you can be. The purpose of making imaginary thinking caps is to help us learn about our own thinking, and to help us think of ways we would like to make our thinking better.

"Your thinking cap will be specially designed to help you through all kinds of difficult thinking situations, and it will lead you on all kinds of exciting thinking adventures.

"But the first thing you must do before you draw your thinking cap is to think about your own thinking, to discover how you want your thinking cap to help you."

Ms. Greenway's students look puzzled.

"Let me give you an example. When I think about my own thinking, I see that sometimes my thinking is a little disorganized. For instance right now I have lots of ideas about thinking caps, but they are getting jumbled up in my mind; sometimes I don't sort things out, and I end up feeling confused. So my thinking cap will have a special feature on it, to help me be less disorganized. Now if you were helping me design my thinking cap, what would you put on it, to help me make my thinking less disorganized?"

A student raises her hand.

"I know. You could put a little buzzer on your cap that reminds you to write things down or make a list."

She agrees that that's a good idea and asks for other suggestions. After a few more comments from students, she continues:

"Well, I can see we're going to have some pretty creative thinking caps on Friday. But here's what I want us to do first. All week we're going to pay especially close attention to our thinking, so we can discover ways we want our thinking caps to help us. This week, I'm going to ask you lots of questions about your thinking, and give you plenty of time to think about your thinking. We'll start now.

"Close your eyes and think back to last week in school. See if you can remember a time when you had to think very hard about something. Try to remember what your thinking was like when you were thinking hard. Then, try to imagine how you could have made your thinking better at that time. What could you have done to make yourself be a better thinker?"

Ms. Greenway gives students a moment of quiet time to reflect. Then she goes on.

"Now, turn to your neighbor and tell him or her about the time you remember, and what you could have done to make your thinking better. In a friendly way, see if you can help each other. Can you suggest interesting ways each of you could have made your thinking better?"

Over the course of the week, Ms. Greenway gives her students plenty of opportunities to reflect on their own thinking and to come to know themselves as thinkers. For example, she asks them to reflect on their thinking after they've taken a quiz, written a report, solved a puzzle, and worked in small groups. At first she thought it would be difficult to find opportunities to encourage reflection, but it turns out to be surprisingly easy: Any time she wants her students to *think* is also a time when she can ask her students to reflect on their thinking.

On Friday, she makes sure to have craft paper, markers, and other drawing implements on hand for students to use when drawing their thinking caps. As students work, she is delighted at their creativity and insight. She sees that her students really have come to know themselves better as thinkers. For example, one student who is chronically late has built a "be on time" reminder into his thinking cap. A timid student has invented a pink "bravery button" to push when she wants to speak up in class. And these are just a few of the ideas! Some other innovations Ms. Greenway finds include: whistles to announce good ideas; filing systems for school subject matters; spiders' webs to tie ideas together; reward systems to motivate thinking (usually toy- or candy-driven); special eyeglasses to help you concentrate; special hearing aids to make you listen better. Of course, there are the intentionally silly ideas, too. But Ms. Greenway tries to reinforce the positive and avoids rewarding nonserious efforts with too much attention. At the end of the lesson, Ms. Greenway posts students' drawings on the classroom wall—they make quite a vivid display!

Overall, Ms. Greenway is struck by how able her students are to step back from their own thinking and think about how to manage it better. She had feared they might turn out to be developmentally unready for this, but clearly she was mistaken. She resolves to keep the spirit of mental management alive in her classroom by finding ways to help students use their thinking cap ideas productively.

Meeting the Bottom Lines

In this example, Ms. Greenway touches on all four of the bottom lines mentioned in the previous chapter.

Bottom Line: Model mental management.   yes ■ no □

Ms. Greenway briefly models an aspect of mental management when she talks to her students about how her own thinking can be disorganized and what she would like her thinking cap to do for her.

Bottom Line: Explain key mental management concepts and practices. yes ■ no □

Although this vignette does not emphasize explanation around mental management, explanation does have a presence. Ms. Greenway begins the activity by straightforwardly explaining to students the purpose of making imaginary thinking caps: it is, she says, to help them become more aware of their own thinking and of ways they would like it to be better.

Also, by placing students' drawings of their thinking caps on the classroom wall, Ms. Greenway ensures that pictorial explanations of ideas about mental management provide a visible reminder, keeping the idea of mental management a presence in the classroom.

Bottom Line: Organize opportunities for student/student and teacher/student interactions about mental management.   yes ■ no □

Ms. Greenway has built an interactive element into the thinking cap activity by asking students to talk with a partner about thinking challenges they remember. By doing this, she is making talk about thought an ordinary part of classroom discourse.

Bottom Line: Make sure that students get feedback about their mental management practices.   yes ■   no □

Simply by providing class time over the course of the week for students to reflect on their thinking, and by asking for reflection in the context of regular classroom activities like taking a quiz and working in groups, Ms. Greenway is providing positive reinforcement for the idea of mental management: she is showing that it is valued in her classroom. She also provides positive and informative feedback about students' posters.

Following Up: Integrating the Lesson into the Classroom Culture

Ms. Greenway has posted students' thinking cap drawings on the classroom wall: They help keep the idea of mental management fresh in her and her students' minds. Over the next several weeks as she's teaching her regular lessons, she makes a special effort to provide students with time to reflect on their own thinking—to talk about it and to write about it. As well as reacting to what they write from time to time, she has them talk with and advise one another about their ideas; thus her students get occasional feedback from her and frequent feedback from one another. In these ways, she shows students that mental management will continue to be valued in this classroom. Ms. Greenway also tries to use the phrase "mental management" frequently, because she knows what a powerful cultural role language plays in keeping ideas alive. For example, as students are working on a project, she will remind them to be good mental managers and to recall the advice on their thinking caps.

Because Ms. Greenway's focus on mental management is relatively new, she doesn't remember to incorporate it into her teaching as much as she would like. But the drawings on the wall help remind her, and she tries to take advantage of on-the-fly opportunities that occur to her unexpectedly. For example, sometimes in the middle of a lesson she will suddenly take the opportunity to ask students to talk with a partner about their thinking, thereby fostering cultural interaction around mental management. In these and similar ways Ms. Greenway keeps the practice of mental management alive, and it gradually becomes part of the everyday culture of her classroom.

FOURTHOUGHT: A MENTAL MANAGEMENT STRATEGY

The following example is a bit longer than usual, but we describe Four-Thought in detail for two reasons. One, it is a general mental management strategy. It can be used with virtually any thinking challenge, so you will easily be able to imagine using it in a classroom (Tishman, Goodrich, & Mirman Owen, 1990). Two, FourThought can be usefully broken apart. Each of the four steps is a kind of ministrategy that can be put to work on its own. In fact, teachers rarely use all aspects of all four steps at once.

For each step we first describe the purpose of the step and then provide an illustration of use in a high school classroom by showing how a music teacher guides her students through it. Here is a picture of the entire Four-Thought Strategy. In the same way that a picture frame surrounds a picture, the strategy steps of FourThought surround a thinking challenge.

1.

Before Thinking

Get Ready

2.

During Thinking

Set Goals and Standards

Any

Thinking

Challenge

Here

3.

During Thinking

Keep Track of Thinking

4.

After Thinking

Reflect

Step One: Before Thinking—Get Ready

Just as an athlete takes time for mental preparation before an event, the good thinker takes steps to evoke an appropriate frame of mind prior to engaging in a thinking task. This needn't take long—perhaps only half a minute. But it is very important. Create a prepared and fertile state of mind by:

- taking a moment of quiet time
- visualizing the upcoming topic of thought

Example: Get Ready for a Quiz on Early American Music

Points of Style	Narrative
The teacher makes sure students have a picture of the FourThought strategy in view.	Students are about to take a quiz on early American music. The teacher has drawn the FourThought frame on the blackboard, and written "early American music" inside, where the thinking challenge goes.
She directs their attention to step 1 . . .	"Let's be good mental managers on this quiz," she tells students, "by using the FourThought strategy. You've used it before, so you know what to do. Let's start with step 1."
. . . and gives students time to get ready.	"Take the next minute," she says, "to quietly focus your mind on the thinking you're about to do. Take a few deep breaths. . . . Clear your mind of any clutter."
Then, she helps students to vividly picture the upcoming topic.	"Try to form a mental image of the topic. Ask yourself: 'Who is playing these instruments? What do the instruments look like?'"
	"'Who is listening to the music? Where is the music being played?'"

Step Two: During Thinking—Set Goals and Standards

Good thinking establishes goals and standards. Goals and standards concern what one wants to achieve and the criteria for achieving it. For example, in writing a book report students might set goals such as capturing key points, painting a vivid picture of the book, and sparking readers' interest. The good mental manager articulates her thinking goals and sets standards to help her tell whether she has met those goals. A standard for writing an imaginative book report, for instance, might be to look at things from an unusual point of view. So being a mental manager during thinking means:

- setting goals
- using standards

Early American Music Quiz, continued

Points of Style	Narrative
The teacher moves to step 2 of the strategy and prompts students to articulate their goals.	"Now let's move to step 2," the teacher says. "What are your goals in taking this quiz?"
	"To get a good grade," a student answers. "Okay, that's fine. And what else?"

"Well," says another student, "one of my goals is to think through the questions carefully, because I know I tend to rush things, and I need *time* to give good answers."

"A goal for me," says another student, "is to write some *interesting* answers."

Teacher helps students find standards to use, to guide them in meeting their goals.

The teacher lists students' goals on the blackboard. Soon she turns to the question of standards.

"What standards will you use to meet your goals?" she asks.

"Work slow and don't rush," one student answers.

"Try to keep a picture in my mind of these instruments," another student says, "because if I can *see* them, it's easier to say something interesting about them."

She helps students keep goals and standards in the forefront of their minds, by writing all ideas on the board.

Students continue to think of standards, and the teacher writes them on the board. She explains a few standards she herself thinks are important (for example to check for spelling errors), then tells students to begin the quiz.

Step Three: During Thinking—Keep Track of Thinking

This step looks small, but it is very important! It tells the thinker to do some "on-line monitoring"—to keep track of how, and how well, standards and goals are being met. Often we get caught up in the fray of thinking and forget to stand back to check on how we are doing. This is especially important in a school setting, where students' anxiety about grades and the like can cause them to become fixed on an often fruitless path. Keeping track of thinking means:

- periodically monitoring how well you are meeting your goals
- remembering to play the role of mental manager

Early American Music, Continued

Points of Style   Narrative

At step 3, the teacher reminds students to monitor their thinking as they go.

As students work, the teacher periodically reminds them to keep track of how well they are meeting their goals and standards.

She reminds them to check that they are meeting their goals and standards and reminds them to play the role of mental manager.

Every ten minutes or so, she says something like: "Stand back for a moment and ask yourself: 'How am I doing? Am I meeting my goals? Am I meeting my standards?' "

She also reminds students to play the role of mental manager. "Don't forget that you are your own mental managers," she says. "You want to think hard, of course, but also ask yourself: 'How is the *direction* of my thinking?' "

Step Four: After Thinking—Reflect

Any good manager takes time to review, and learn from, experience. So it is with the good mental manager. As their own mental managers, students need to learn to regularly ask themselves such questions as: Where was my thinking strong? Where was it weak? How well did I meet my goals? Which standards were easy to fulfill; which were hard? What improvements could I make in my thinking next time? Asking themselves these kinds of questions helps students learn about—and from—their own thinking, and reminds them that they themselves are in charge of making their thinking as good as it can be. Accordingly, after finishing a thinking challenge, students should:

- review and evaluate thinking
- look for improvements

Early American Music, Concluded

Points of Style

Narrative

Finally at step 4 the teacher asks students to reflect on their thinking, emphasizing that the discussion is not about the answers to the quiz, but about how their thinking went.

"So," the teacher asks her students when the quiz is over, "how did your thinking go? Don't ask me questions about the right answers—think back for a moment on the thinking you just did, and ask yourself: 'What parts of your thinking were hard? What parts were easy? How well did you meet your standards and goals?' "

After a moment, one student raises his hand.

"A standard I had at the beginning was to work slow and not rush," he said. "I did okay, but I did rush a few times, so it was hard to meet that standard."

She emphasizes <u>self-</u>
evaluation . . .

"Was your thinking better when you worked more slowly?" the teacher asked. "Was working slow a *good* standard to have?"

"Yeah, it was. 'Cause when I answered the questions slowly, I got more ideas."

Other students raise their hands, and the teacher continues the discussion. She directs students to think about improvements in their thinking.

. . . and prompts students to
come up with their own ideas
about improvements they
could make in their thinking
next time.

"What could you do next time," she asks, "to make your thinking even better?"

"I could have studied more . . . ha . . . ha . . ." one student says, cynically.

"That's important to realize," the teacher responds. "How much you study is certainly something you have control over. Other ideas?"

"Next time I would look over the whole quiz first, to see how many questions there were on it, and what they were like," a student answered.

"Me, too," another student joined in. "I forgot to do that this time, and I then ran out of time.

"That sounds like a helpful improvement," says the teacher, "let's see if we can think of three more improvements, and then we'll take a break."

Meeting the Bottom Lines

This lesson, structured around the FourThought strategy, meets most of the bottom lines for incorporating mental management into the classroom culture.

Bottom Line: Model mental management. yes ☐ no ■

This example of FourThought doesn't show the teacher modeling mental management. Of course, the students are already familiar with the strategy. In introducing it, the teacher would have modeled it.

Bottom Line: Explain key mental management concepts and practices.
yes ■ no ☐

Although the students are already familiar with the strategy, as the teacher leads them through the activity, she does provide some explanation about each step.

Bottom Line: Organize opportunities for student/student and teacher/student interactions around mental management. yes ■ no ☐

Ultimately, students will be taking the quiz solo. But the teacher makes sure that there is plenty of class discussion (a kind of interaction) around aspects of the strategy, particularly the setting of goals and standards (step 2).

Bottom Line: Make sure that students get feedback about their mental management practices. yes ■ no ☐

Feedback is present here in two ways. First of all, step four of FourThought directs students to reflect on and evaluate their own thinking, thus building self-feedback into the strategy itself. Second, the teacher conducts a discussion about students' thoughts at step 4, thus creating an opportunity to provide feedback by reinforcing student insights about thinking.

How to Use FourThought

As mentioned earlier, FourThought is really several ministrategies clustered together. As a single grand strategy, it is a powerful tool for managing complex or lengthy thinking challenges—challenges such as preparing a report, taking a quiz, planning a presentation, designing and implementing a project, making an important decision, solving a complex problem. In the above example, the whole of FourThought was used in a single lesson. Alternatively, the strategy can be stretched over several lessons. For example, students might use FourThought to help them manage their thinking while planning and building a project for the Science Fair. The *before thinking* step would help them conscientiously get ready at the beginning of the project; the *during thinking* steps would help them to set goals and standards and keep track of their thinking as they went along; and the *after thinking* step would help them to reflect carefully on their thinking at the end of the project.

Following Up: Integrating FourThought into the Classroom Culture

Because it is visually evocative, a poster of the FourThought thinking frame on the classroom wall functions well as a constantly present explanation: it is a powerful way to keep the message of FourThought on students' minds. Modeling at the outset and occasional modeling along the way are also important elements. For example, while assigning a history chapter to read as homework, a teacher can model what it looks like to set and follow standards for the reading task (FourThought step 2). Another way to blend FourThought into the classroom culture, of course, is to create interactive episodes about one or several of the FourThought steps, as illustrated in the above example. Finally, and very importantly, interaction and feedback around FourThought can be cultivated by asking students to coach each other in the FourThought strategy steps and by encouraging them to use the language of FourThought (e.g., "before thinking, get ready") with the teacher, and with each other.

MODELING MENTAL MANAGEMENT: AN EXAMPLE IN REAL TIME

The amateur psychologist in José Puntes knows how important it is for adults to model good thinking practices for children. The savvy sixth-grade teacher in him also knows that children aren't easily fooled by idealized or sterile examples of such practices. For example, he has found that if he models for students flawless and frustration-free decision making, his students quickly lose interest, failing to see a connection between the rather messy decision-making dilemmas they experience in their own lives and his too-perfect demonstration. On the other hand, if he shows students the genuine frustration in his own thinking that comes from puzzling long and hard over a decision, *and* he models ways to get beyond that frustration, his students perk right up.

Mr. Puntes takes this insight about real-time modeling to heart in his everyday teaching. He models his own mental management thinking processes frequently for students, in order to reveal what adult thinking looks like. And when he does, he tries to avoid displays of sugar-coated or unrealistic thinking. Rather, he aims to show how good thinking faces and surmounts the real and sometimes very personal difficulties that all thinkers, adults and young people alike, are likely to face.

Mr. Puntes particularly likes to work with his students on good decision making. He knows that students have difficulty making decisions, and although sometimes their decisions seem small to the adult eye (what movie to see, what after-school activity to choose, who to get together with on Saturday), these can be decisions of moment to children, and also a training ground for adult decision-making practices.

There are lots of natural obstacles to good decision making—impulsivity, shortsightedness, bias, to name just a few—and decision making can be dramatically enhanced by good mental management. Here is an example of how Mr. Puntes models mental management and decision making for his students, without glossing over the hard parts. One day in the third week of the school year, Mr. Puntes came to class with this to say:

> *This week, you all have at least two important decisions to make. As you know, this is the week you can choose an after-school activity. Also, this week you'll have to choose a topic for your independent project in social studies. Since it's near the beginning of the school year, you probably have other important decisions to make, too—decisions about who to make friends with and about how to organize your study habits, for example.*
>
> *Today I was thinking about what it was like to make the kinds of hard decisions you'll be making, and I remembered a hard decision I had to make. A few years ago, when I first came to Clairmont School, I wanted to choose an after-school activity to be involved in, as a teacher. I was about to decide to be a soccer coach for the school soccer team, because I've coached soccer before, and I like it. But I realized I was about to make an impulsive decision. By "impulsive" I mean I was just rushing into a decision without taking time to really think it through. So I reminded myself to be a good mental manager, and to think about my thinking. "Whoa," I said to myself. "Hold your horses. Take a minute to be thoughtful about this decision." I realized that I hadn't considered other options. Coaching soccer was the first idea that popped into my head. But there were other things I was interested in, too. So I asked myself, what else I could do after school? I reminded myself to use my imagination to think of unusual ideas. I also remembered that it helps to put ideas on paper, so I made a little diagram like this:*

Mr. Puntes drew this diagram on the blackboard.

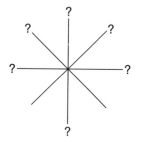

Then he went on:

After a while I had written an idea at each point of the star, and had found two or three ideas that seemed interesting. Coaching soccer was one idea, of course. Another idea I had was starting a chess club (I bet you didn't know I liked chess, did you?). I had a few other interesting ideas, too. But to be honest, I remember that at this point, I was feeling a little impatient, and I was again inclined to just rush into a decision—to be impulsive— without taking time to think. After all, thinking can be hard work, and I was getting tired! But I tried to be a good mental manager and reminded myself to think about the pros and cons for each idea, before I decided which idea was best. For example, a "pro" for coaching soccer was that I had done it before, so I knew how to do it. But this was also a "con," because I was in the mood to learn something new and soccer was old hat to me. After a bit more thinking time, I finally made what I believe was a very good decision. I think you all know what my decision was, don't you? I decided to help students start a school newspaper. And I'm glad to say that our own Clairmont School Gazette *is, in my opinion, one of finest school news-papers in this state!*

So there you are. You've just had a glimpse of what my thinking looks like when I try to be a good mental manager about making decisions. I'm sure you noticed that it takes lots of work—and lots of time—to be a good thinker. But it is well worth the effort, and I hope you'll try to be good mental managers when you are making your important decisions this week. Oh, and by the way. When you are making a decision about what after-school activity to pursue, you might keep in mind the thrill and excitement of spending some after-school hours working on the school newspaper. Only as one of the many options you thoughtfully consider, of course . . .

Meeting the Bottom Lines

It was Mr. Puntes' intention to demonstrate mental management by exam-ple, so his lesson principally addressed the modeling and explanation bot-tom lines.

Bottom Line: Model mental management. yes ■ no ☐

The main point of this vignette is to show how one teacher models thinking for his students. By describing his thinking aloud, Mr. Puntes is providing his students with a richly detailed model of what good thinking looks like. Such a description can serve as a guide to students in two ways. It provides students with a model of how to talk about their own thinking, and it shows them what it looks like to be a good mental manager when making deci-sions. Note that Mr. Puntes also provides his students with a visual model of good mental management, when he draws a diagram on the blackboard showing how he graphically organized his thinking.

Bottom Line: Explain key mental management concepts and practices. yes ■ no ☐

Very often, the cultural forces in the classroom weave together in a single activity or episode. Such is the case here. Mr. Puntes does not stop with modeling the process; he explains various aspects of it too. In fact, it is a good practice to accompany models with an explanation much of the time, since students don't always get the point from a model alone.

Bottom Line: Organize opportunities for student/student and teacher/student interactions around mental management. yes ☐ no ■

It is not Mr. Puntes' intent to engage students interactively in this particular lesson.

Bottom Line: Make sure that students get feedback about their mental management practices. yes ☐ no ■

Providing students with feedback is not the main intent of this lesson either.

Mr. Puntes's story gives us a picture of how a teacher can reveal and model the thinking processes involved in mental management in a way that underscores the real challenges and obstacles to good thinking. In this case, Mr. Puntes modeled how good mental management can meet the obstacle of impulsivity in decision making—a challenge for all decision makers, not only young ones.

Mental management can be modeled around many thinking challenges students face every day. For example, teachers can model how to manage the thinking processes behind good study habits, thoughtful reading, and effective writing. The important thing is to acknowledge, rather than gloss over, the real difficulties inherent in good thinking.

Many obstacles to good thinking occur in the form of fearful or negative emotions—such as the feeling of impulsivity, feelings of confusion or bewilderment, a fear of failure, a fear of looking foolish, the feeling of being overwhelmed. Other challenges to good thinking concern dispositional tendencies like closed-mindedness, one-dimensional thinking, and disorganized thinking. There is no such thing as a perfect human thinker who never experiences any of these obstacles or challenges. Good teacher modeling takes into account the obstacles that all thinkers experience and shows how good mental managers can use realistic tactics to surmount them.

Following Up: Integrating the Example into the Classroom Culture

Mr. Puntes can follow up his demonstration of mental management and decision making in many different ways. For example, if he wanted to emphasize direct instruction in the culture of mental management, he might conduct a lesson in which students reflected on their own decision making (perhaps while working in pairs, to encourage student/student interaction and feedback). Taking a longer view, he can make sure to be an ongoing cultural model by continuing to model mental management around different kinds of thinking challenges, not just decision making. In fact, many thinking challenges that students face everyday present modeling opportunities. For example, Mr. Puntes might model how to manage the thinking behind good study habits, behind thoughtful reading, and behind effective writing. In whatever Mr. Puntes does, he wants to continue to acknowledge, rather than gloss over, the real difficulties inherent in good thinking.

TAKING THE PLUNGE: GUIDELINES FOR INSTRUCTION

If you have found the ideas in this chapter powerful, you may be interested in incorporating instruction in mental management into your own classroom culture.

Here are a couple of instructional "plunge points"—good points of departure for introducing mental management into the classroom that you can use immediately, even if you don't yet feel fully knowledgeable about the concept of mental management. By all means use your own approach if you have a clear sense of how you'd like to begin. Or read over the two plunge points below and choose the one that you judge will work best for you and your students.

Plunge Point #1

1. Reread the example "Put on Your Thinking Cap" earlier in this chapter and use Ms. Greenway's activity as a guide for designing your own lesson.

2. Find a time at the beginning of the week to introduce the idea of a thinking cap to your students. Explain that at the end of the week, they will draw pictures of their ideal thinking cap. Make sure that in the introduction you model your own thinking, as Ms. Greenway did when she explained that sometimes her thinking gets jumbled. (You can use Ms. Greenway's example as your own, if it works for you.)

3. Identify several points in the upcoming week when you can ask students to reflect on their own thinking, as Ms. Greenway did.

4. On Friday, conduct a full lesson in which students recall their reflections from the past week and use the information they gained to design and draw their ideal thinking caps. Have on hand creative materials for students to use, such as colored markers, pencils, and craft paper.

5. Reflect. At this point, you have taken the plunge and will likely have a clearer sense of what teaching mental management is all about. So take a few minutes to reflect on your new understanding.

- Review how your conception of mental management has grown over the past week. Ask yourself, what were the classroom or planning events that really made the concept come alive for you?
- Ask yourself what seem to be students' mental management strengths and weaknesses. When does self-reflection seem to come easily to them? When is it difficult, and why?

Plunge Point #2

1. Reread the "FourThought" example earlier in this chapter and use it as a guide in designing your own series of lessons.

2. Choose an important or extended thinking task students will face shortly around which the FourThought strategy can be used. An important task might be taking a quiz or writing an essay. An extended task is one that students must complete over a period of days or even weeks. Some suitable tasks include: planning and conducting an experiment, writing a book report, producing a play, doing an independent project, researching a report, writing a story, making a sculpture, preparing a presentation.

3. Make a poster of the FourThought frame like the one earlier and plan a time to introduce and explain it to students.

4. Identify several points over the next few weeks that correspond to the task you've selected and the four steps of FourThought. For example, if students will be writing a report, identify a time before beginning the report for students to do the "Get Ready" step (step 1), then a time early on in their research to do the "Goals and Standards" step (step 2). Once they are well into the report, find times to remind students to "Keep Track of Thinking" (step 3), and when the report is complete, identify a time for students to do the "Reflect" step (step 4). Use the four sections of the earlier FourThought example as a guide to teaching each of the strategy steps.

5. Reflect. After you've introduced FourThought and taught the first one or two strategy steps, take a minute to consolidate your new understanding of mental management by reflecting on your experience so far.

CONTINUING ON: MAKING MENTAL MANAGEMENT A PERMANENT PART OF THE CLASSROOM CULTURE

Suppose you have taken the mental management plunge, either by using one of the plunge points above or by experimenting on your own. Where do you go from here? How can you keep mental management alive in ongoing, everyday classroom activities?

The key is to weave mental management into the rhythm of regular instruction by attending to the four cultural forces in the classroom—models, explanation, interaction, and feedback. Here are some suggestions about how to put these forces to work in the service of mental management.

Models of Mental Management

- Demonstrate mental management for students. As a teacher, you can demonstrate several different aspects of mental management by reflecting aloud on different thinking occasions. For example, teachers can reflect aloud about how they have handled a hard decision or a sticky problem. They can reflect aloud about how to improve their thinking and about what thinking pitfalls to watch out for. The main purpose of teacher modeling is to provide students with a picture, or model, of mental management so they can have a realistic image of what it might look like when they try it on their own.
- Show students examples of people thinking about their thinking. Artists, scientists, writers, and other kinds of thinkers often write about their reflections on the thinking involved in their craft. Also, professionals in the local community are often quite willing to visit classrooms and talk about the thinking involved in their fields. For example, a local politician might talk about the decision making. Scholars in different fields can be invited to talk about the kind of thinking involved in anthropology, psychology, science, and so on.

Explanation of Mental Management

- Directly teach lessons around mental management tactics and strategies. Direct instruction in mental management includes any teaching activity which aims to impart a mental management skill or proficiency. Often, direct instruction overlaps with other aspects of enculturation. For example, one might teach a lesson in which students work together, coaching each other to reflect on their thinking after completing a group project. The lesson emphasizes student/student cultural interaction, and, as a direct instructional technique, also teaches self-feedback. Other kinds of direct instruction in mental management include the teaching of mental management strategies (for example, FourThought, or any of its substrategies), and the teaching of mental self-awareness tactics (for example, the thinking cap lesson described earlier).

- Incorporate visual mental management cues into the classroom environment. Posters and similar devices serve as ever-present reminders of mental management activities and practices. Even a simple slogan on a bulletin board that says "Think about your thinking!" can be a powerful visual prompt to self-reflection. Two examples of visual mental management cues in this chapter are: Ms. Greenway's students' thinking cap drawings (when they are displayed on the walls they remind students of their own self-generated thinking ideals), and the FourThought poster that illustrates a four-step mental management strategy.

- Integrate mental management components into regular classroom activities. Most straightforwardly, simply provide students with a format and time for reflecting on their thinking after they have completed a regular activity (see FourThought step 4). Or, before a quiz or worksheet, ask students to "get ready" to think by reviewing how they will handle the upcoming task (see FourThought step 1). Another option is to write mental management questions directly into assignments. For example, as students write a compare/contrast essay, add to the task a question that asks them about the standards they will apply to their thinking as they write (see FourThought step 2).

Mental Management Interactions

- Make mental management language a part of everyday classroom discourse. Mental management carries with it a certain style of talking. Usually classroom discourse is about the content of instruction—about what the history text says, and what spelling words are on the quiz. The language of mental management talks about the mental processes involved in think about content. For example, it involves talk about one's thinking behind and around the reading of the history text, and behind and around the taking of a spelling quiz. Using mental management language in the classroom means including in instruction questions that are directly about thinking. For example, if students have been assigned a chapter on the China Trade for homework, in addition to asking them about the content of the reading, ask questions like: "What was your thinking like as you were reading? Did you use any mental management techniques to keep your mind focused? What could you have done to make your thinking about the chapter even sharper?"

- Engage students in cooperative activities around mental management. Too often, self-reflection remains a private affair. This is unfortunate, because peer-assisted self-reflection is a very powerful way to build mental management skills. For instance, in the thinking cap example earlier, Ms. Greenway engaged students in peer-assisted reflection by asking pairs of students to help each other recall and articulate ways to make their thinking better. She did this because she appreciates the force of the truism "I don't know what I think until I hear what I say," and realizes that to a large extent, students must verbalize their reflections aloud in order to really know what they are.

Some well-known cooperative mental management activities include reciprocal teaching in which students help one another build and articulate their thinking around reading strategies (Palincsar & Brown, 1984) and pair problem solving, in which pairs of students coach one another to talk aloud as they work through math problems (Whimbey & Lochhead, 1982).

Here is a simple but effective cooperative mental management activity that can be appended to the end of almost any regular classroom activity. At the close of a lesson, engage students in cooperative thinking by simply asking them to turn to their neighbor and take a minute to describe the thinking they just did: What was hard about it? What was easy? How could it be made better?

- Honor and expect *time* for reflection. Not all interactions in the classroom are verbal. Something as seemingly small as the amount of time one expects students to take before answering a question is a significant kind of cultural interaction, because it carries with it a message about how long people are expected to reflect on things. Studies have shown that students' responses to teachers' questions deepen and improve dramatically when teachers give all students just a few extra seconds to think before taking any answers. Giving thinking time—whether it is extra seconds after a question or extra minutes to quietly reflect after an activity—is a particularly important part of mental management, because thinking about thinking really *does* take time. Try to establish classroom norms that honor and expect this. Encourage cultural interactions around "think time" that involve providing time for thinking during discussions and activities, expecting that others will provide time for thinking in their interactions with their peers, and modeling giving thinking time oneself.

Feedback on Mental Management

- Ask about and comment on students' mental management practices. Usually classroom questions probe students' knowledge about content. Asking students questions about their thinking *processes*—questions such as "how did you come up with that idea?" or "what steps did you take to solve that problem?"—creates opportunities to provide students with informative feedback about how to better manage their thinking. The feedback can take the form of providing advice; for example, a teacher might give a student advice about how to do a better job of setting thinking goals. And it can also take the form of positive reinforcement, such as when a teacher commends a student for doing a good job of reflecting on and evaluating her own thinking.

• Build mental management into regular assessments. Whether we intend it or not, students see assessments as judgments, and thus experience them as feedback. Teachers can make use of this, by incorporating mental management tasks into standard quizzes and tests, and responding to them informatively. For example, a social studies quiz might close with these two metacognitive questions: (1) what part of your thinking on this quiz went well? and (2) what part was difficult? The teacher can then provide feedback to students about their responses, reinforcing good mental management practices and noting areas for improvement. Also, of course, including mental management tasks in standard assessments sends a positive message to students about their importance.

Checking Your Progress

Table 7.1 on page 74 is a sample weekly chart that is filled out with some possible mental management activities a teacher might have done during the week. It reflects the four cultural forces: models, explanation, interaction, and feedback.

TROUBLESHOOTING: QUESTIONS AND ANSWERS ABOUT MENTAL MANAGEMENT

I've heard that metacognition is a pretty sophisticated thinking skill. Are primary school students, especially students in the early grades, really developmentally capable of mental management as you describe it here?

Yes, they are. Research shows that although mental management is rarely explicitly taught in school, young children are quite able to reflect effectively on their own thinking, given an appropriate learning environment. What this environment must include is lots of opportunities to explore thinking in a relatively open-ended way. This means helping children to become aware of their thinking selves (the thinking cap activity described earlier is a good example of this) and providing real opportunities for them to practice evaluating and guiding their own thinking (FourThought, or any of its substrategies, is one way of creating these kinds of opportunities).

TABLE 7.1 Mental Management Weekly Progress Chart

	MONDAY	TUESDAY	WEDNESDAY	THURSDAY	FRIDAY
Models		I tried to model my thinking, like Mr. Puntes did (in this chapter). It wasn't as good as his, but I think I did O.K.			I keep trying to uncover my own thinking process for them, so I described how I used Four-Thought steps in choosing an upcoming class assignment.
Explanation			I introduced and explained the FourThought strategy.		
Interaction	I had students reflect on their thinking and make thinking caps, like in the example (in this chapter). Students share thoughts with each other.		Together we worked through an example using FourThought, and then students tried it on their own.	Since they were learning about gears, I had them design household inventions using gears and had them use the Four-Thought steps in doing their designs.	I had students explain their gear designs to each other and then describe how it was to think about their thinking.
Feedback	Students gave feedback and suggested ways to help make each other's thinking better.		Students weren't sure how to do it, especially steps 2 and 3, so I gave them feedback to help them.		Students gave each other feedback on their thoughts about thinking.

94

What if when I ask my students to think about their thinking, their minds go blank and they don't have anything to say?

Probably this *will* happen, especially when you first introduce mental management. This is mainly because students are rarely explicitly asked to talk about their own thinking, and they don't have a clear sense of what it's supposed to sound like. One way you can help, of course, is by modeling mental management. Think aloud in front of your students—let them "hear" how your mind works, and how you guide your own thinking.

Another thing to do is ask students *specific* questions about their thinking. For instance, when you ask them to stand back and review their thinking while writing a poem, ask them whether it was hard to write the first line; whether the idea for the poem came full-fledged or whether they had to develop it; whether their thinking stumbled as they were writing (and if so, where?); and so on.

Most importantly, bear with students' momentary silence when you ask them to stand back and think about their thinking, even if it feels uncomfortable at first. *Give thinking time!* Reflecting on thinking takes a good deal more time than the standard two or three seconds we usually wait after asking a student a question. Notice that in the examples in this chapter, teachers provided substantial time for reflection—from thirty seconds up to several minutes—before asking students to articulate their reflections.

If reflecting on thinking takes so much time, won't teaching mental management take time away from subject matter learning?

It depends on how you define subject matter learning. If it is simply the learning of facts you're after, then yes, time for mental management takes time away from content learning. But if you want children to learn how to learn on their own—if you want them to become their own intellectual critics instead of depending on others to tell them how and what to think—then there is no better investment than time spent on mental management.

In fact, most mental management strategies consume relatively little instructional time. For example, systematically asking students to reflect back on their thinking at the end of a thinking task (for example, at the end of a quiz or the close of watching a film) might take only a minute or two of class time, but it has a very high yield in terms of thoughtful learning. Some teachers build mental management tactics into students' homework, for example by asking them to jot down a few sentences describing and evaluating their own thinking at the close of reading a chapter in a text assigned as homework. This saves classroom time, but even more importantly, it encourages students to become autonomous mental managers in their lives outside of school.

▶ 8

The Strategic Spirit

> **Strategic Spirit:** *1. An enthusiasm for systematic thinking. 2. The tendency to invent and use thinking strategies in response to challenging situations.*

There are African legends about a clever monkey who always finds himself in a fix. One Clever Monkey tale goes like this.

Clever Monkey saw a delectable fruit hanging in a tree. He was very hungry, and his first thought was to scramble up the tree and quickly eat it. But then he noticed that the branch from which the fruit hung was quite slender. He saw that his weight would bow the branch over so steeply that he would slide, headlong, off the tree before he could reach the fruit.

Clever Monkey wasn't called clever for nothing, and this was just the kind of problem he liked to solve. So he sat down under the tree and made this plan: First, he would try to think about all the different possible ways he might reach the fruit. Then, he would choose the very best idea—the one that would be most likely to work.

The first idea Clever Monkey thought of was to wait for Uncle Elephant to pass by, so that he could jump on his back and be tall enough to reach the fruit. His second idea was to shake the tree very hard, and hope that the fruit would come loose and fall to the ground. His third idea was to ask Brother Deer for help: Clever Monkey could climb the tree so the branches bent low to the ground, and Brother Deer could reach up and pluck the fruit with his soft mouth.

Which idea was best? Clever Monkey sat and thought. The problem with Uncle Elephant was that the fruit was very high in the tree, and even Uncle Elephant might not be tall enough to reach it. The problem with trying to shake the fruit loose was that the fruit was very delicate: If it fell, it might shatter; then the ants would eat all the fruit, and Clever Monkey would have none. The problem with asking for Brother Deer's help was that Brother Deer would surely be hungry too, and Clever Monkey would be obliged to share his prize with him.

Clever Monkey looked up longingly at the delectable fruit, feeling hungrier and hungrier. He thought about his three ideas. If I wait for Uncle Elephant, he thought, I might never get the fruit. If I shake the tree, I still might never get the fruit. If I ask Brother Deer for help, I will only get half the fruit. Clever Monkey's stomach growled. All things considered, he decided, half a meal is better than none. He ran off to find Brother Deer.

Clever Monkey has what might be called the *strategic spirit*. Faced with a challenging situation, he thinks strategically about what to do, instead of acting impulsively. The strategy he invents is a straightforward three-step problem-solving strategy. He wants the fruit in the tree, but there is no obvious way to reach it. So, step one, he brainstorms alternative solutions. Then, step two, he evaluates each idea. Finally, step three, he prudently chooses the most promising course of action.

Over the last decade or so, a large body of educational research has been amassed that shows what many educators already intuitively know: By almost any measure, students who think strategically tend to do better in school, and tend to be better thinkers in general. While these findings may seem obvious to the thoughtful educator, the literature has also yielded a tremendous wealth of thinking strategies and tactics relevant to children's school lives, along with practical and effective ways to teach these strategies. To a large extent, this chapter is built on this literature.

Already, a fair amount of educational material has been developed that focuses on teaching "ready-made" thinking strategies, that is, prescribed, stepwise strategies that help students tackle important thinking challenges such as problem solving and decision making (Perkins, Goodrich, Tishman, & Owen, 1994). These strategies can indeed be quite useful to students, and we discuss a particularly powerful ready-made decision-making strategy in the following chapter. However, truly learning to be a clever monkey—that is, learning to approach a variety of thinking challenges productively and planfully—means more than just being acquainted with a few good thinking strategies. It also means having the *strategic spirit*—the inclination to be reflective, not impulsive, and to take pleasure in inventing and using stepwise procedures.

The aim of this chapter is to show how to cultivate students' strategic spirit. Shortly, we'll give some examples of what the strategic spirit looks like in the classroom. But first we address the question of what exactly a thinking strategy is.

WHAT IS A THINKING STRATEGY?

A thinking strategy is an explicit and articulate plan for how to thread one's way through an intellectually challenging situation. The kinds of thinking strategies people use and invent are as varied as the intellectual challenges they face: There are decision-making strategies for the challenge of choosing the best course of action; understanding strategies for the challenge of acquiring knowledge; problem-solving strategies for the challenge of working your way out of a pickle; inventive thinking strategies for the challenge of building a better mousetrap. For more specific challenges, there are reading strategies, studying strategies, test-taking strategies, writing strategies, and math problem-solving strategies. And even more specifically, there are algebra strategies, chess strategies, medical diagnosis strategies, courtroom defense strategies, improve-your-assertiveness strategies, and Scrabble strategies. Despite their varying levels of generality, what all of these strategies have in common is that they are stepwise (but not necessarily rigid) procedures that are intentionally executed by the thinker, in order to achieve a desired goal.

WHAT IS THE STRATEGIC SPIRIT?

Suppose you are an eighth-grade social studies teacher, teaching a unit on the Renaissance in Europe. You have just asked your students to do an independent project on any aspect of the Renaissance they choose—art, architecture, trade, daily life, anything at all. Their task is simply to choose a topic, research it, and prepare a small report or presentation.

Teachers who have done independent projects with their students before will recognize the kind of students who have quite a difficult time choosing a topic on their own, despite the latitude you've offered, or maybe because of it! These students strain hard to come up with an idea they like, but their search for good ideas consists simply of effortful concentration, as if with sufficient concentration the right idea would suddenly "pop." Perhaps because this approach *is* so effortful, students who think this way tend to give up easily. They soon come to you, pleading help: "I can't think of a good topic. . . . *You* tell me what I should do." This is because such students sometimes approach the task of finding ideas as a "mental muscle" type of challenge. Here is an alternative approach.

Imagine a student who has had some instruction in thinking strategies and approaches the task of finding ideas as a strategic challenge. Being familiar with some basic thinking strategy tactics, this student *plans* how to search for a good idea. Working on paper, first he writes down the word *goal*. He thinks for a minute about what his goal is: He wants a good idea for an independent project, of course—something that will earn him a good grade.

But he also wants to find a topic about which there is ample information. And, above all, he wants a topic that is interesting, intriguing—one that will hold his interest. He writes these goals down, then writes a second word down on the paper: *ideas.* Under this word, he makes a list of the numbers one through eight, with a space after each number. He figures he should be able to brainstorm at least eight possible topics. (He writes the numbers down because he knows that it helps to give yourself quotas to fill when looking for ideas, otherwise you tend to give up too soon.) He brainstorms eight possible independent topics. Some are interesting, a few are pretty weak. Then, he reviews his list and circles the three ideas that seem the most promising. He quickly runs through the pros and cons of each circled idea, keeping his original goals in mind, and asking himself such questions as, Will I find enough information about this topic? Will it hold my interest? Finally, he chooses an idea that he thinks is imaginative and interesting, and goes to check it with the teacher.

This student, ideal though he may be, has the *strategic spirit.* He recognizes a thinking challenge, makes a plan, then carries it out. Now clearly, most students (and adults) aren't like this, nor are they likely to be, without plenty of encouragement and instruction in the use of thinking strategies. In fact, people's thinking in many challenging situations is often *counter*-strategic: It is either impulsive (such as when people respond to a challenge by plunging ahead without taking time to plan), or effortful but directionless (like the "mental muscle" kind of thinking described above).

Teachers can cultivate the strategic spirit by helping students recognize their own impulsive or effortful reactions to thinking challenges and to show them that an alternative way of thinking is possible. One powerful way to do this is also particularly straightforward: When strategic thinking is appropriate, teachers can ask students for a *strategy,* rather than asking for an immediate answer.

Here is an example. Suppose that instead of immediately asking students for an idea about an independent project, the teacher of the Renaissance unit asked her students to *plan* how to find a good topic. Here's how the classroom discussion might go:

Teacher: As you know, for the next two weeks, you'll be working on an independent project of your choice: the only constraint is that it must have something to do with the Renaissance. Now, you all probably want to find a really great idea for a topic, and to find a really great idea takes time. You need a *strategy.* Can anyone think of a *strategic* way to find a good idea?

Student #1: What do you mean by strategic?

Teacher: Strategic means *planful.* A thinking strategy is a plan that consists of a series of steps you take to meet a goal. There, now I've given you a clue about an important strategic "step." *(Students are silent, and the teacher goes on.)* The clue is the word *goal*. Maybe the first thing we should do to find a good idea is to state our goal precisely—say exactly what we want our good idea to be like. So let's state our goal. What would be "good" about a good idea for an independent project?

Student #2: Well, to be good, it would have to interesting. *(The teacher writes the word "goal" on the blackboard, and underneath it writes: "idea should be interesting.")*

Student #3: And you want to make sure you can find books about it. I once picked this really interesting idea for a project in science class, on termites. But I could hardly find any information on them.

The teacher writes "you should be able to find information on the topic" on the blackboard, then collects a few more ideas about goals. Eventually, she moves on and asks students to think what the next strategy step should be. With some help, students come up with the idea that they should brainstorm lots of ideas about possible topics—including creative and unusual ideas—before they select one. They do this, and then they each carefully choose an idea that they like. After the discussion, the teacher asks students to identify the steps in the strategy that they invented and used. With students' help, she writes this on the board:

STRATEGY FOR FINDING A GOOD INDEPENDENT PROJECT TOPIC

Step 1. State your goals
Step 2. Brainstorm lots of ideas
Step 3. Carefully choose the best idea

Strategy Building Blocks

As the above example suggests, acquiring the strategic spirit involves learning about strategy *steps*. Interestingly, although there are innumerable opportunities to use thinking strategies—from problem solving and decision making, to studying and spelling—most strategies consist of variations on four core strategic steps, or "building blocks." Just as you can construct many different structures from basic building materials like wood, plaster, and concrete, you can build a wide variety of thinking strategies—strategies that address lots of different kinds of thinking challenges—from a core group of four basic strategy steps. The following chapter gives examples of how students can use strategy building blocks to construct their own

TABLE 8.1

Thinking Challenge	Strategy Step (Building Block)
When you need to be clear about what you're doing or where you're going . . .	STATE . . . either the problem, the situation, or your goal(s).
When you need to think broadly about something . . .	SEARCH . . . for ideas, options, possibilities, purposes, features, assumptions, causes, effects, questions, dimensions, hypotheses, facts, or interpretations.
When you need to assess, rate, or decide something . . .	EVALUATE . . . options, plans, ideas, theories, or things.
When you need to think about the details of something . . .	ELABORATE . . . possibilities, plans, options, hypotheses, or ideas.

strategies. For now, Table 8.1 shows an overview of the four strategy building blocks and the specific thinking challenges they address.

These four building blocks or variations of them can be used to build a strategy to meet virtually any thinking challenge. For example, Clever Monkey's problem-solving strategy was built out of the search and evaluate steps; he searched broadly for possible solutions to the problem of retrieving the fruit, then evaluated the solutions and chose the best one. The strategy devised by the students in the example above for finding a good Renaissance project was also built out of strategy building blocks: they stated their goals, searched creatively for lots of options, then carefully evaluated their options and chose one that met their goals.

WHY IS THE STRATEGIC SPIRIT IMPORTANT?

Why focus on cultivating the strategic spirit by teaching students to build strategies themselves, rather than teaching them ready-made strategies, such as a specific problem-solving strategy or decision-making strategy? Ready-made strategies can be tremendously useful of course, and a particularly powerful ready-made strategy is discussed in the following chapter. But it would be folly to ignore the fact that life has a way of confronting us with situations that demand more than ready-made tools and solutions. The truly versatile thinker is one who is able to construct, invent, or modify a thinking strategy to meet the unique demands of the situation at hand. Here are four specific ways that the strategic spirit—the inclination and ability not only to use strategies, but also to invent them—is important to learners.

1. The strategic spirit helps students counter a significant obstacle to good thinking: strenuous but directionless effort. Earlier we mentioned the "mental muscle" approach to thinking. This occurs when students believe that if they simply try very, very hard, somehow the right answer will spring to mind fully formed, like Athena springing from Zeus's thigh. Such an approach does work sometimes. But quite often, students persevere in thinking along a single track uselessly, strenuously working their minds, but working them along the wrong path. An example of this is when students try and try to solve a math problem by long division, when really what they need to do is think about using another mathematical operation altogether.

In general, mental effort is like many other resources. It is potentially valuable, but it should be thoughtfully channeled. What students need to be able to do is to stand back and make a plan to tackle the problem strategically. They require a plan that will prompt them to search broadly for alternative approaches and help them to track their thinking as they go along, keeping alert for dead ends. This inclination to stand back and construct a plan, together with an ability to use appropriate steps, is what the strategic spirit is all about.

2. The strategic spirit energizes learning. It does so because using a thinking strategy is a powerful way of engaging with a subject matter. Consider the difference between passively listening to a lecture about Alexander the Great's decision to make war on Persia and inventing a strategy to creatively think through Alexander's situation yourself—a strategy to think broadly about his goals and options and what you might have done in his stead. Certainly, the latter activity is likely to be more engaging. In short, the strategic spirit energizes learning because it helps students to inquire deeply, creatively, and independently into diverse areas of knowledge.

3. The strategic spirit fosters independent thinking. By constructing and using thinking strategies, learners find themselves in situations where they must plan for themselves what course of action to take and how to take it. Cultivating the strategic spirit in the classroom breaks set with the traditional notion that knowledge is something the teacher "has" and that the learner must passively "receive." Rather, it makes learning and knowing the result of the planful and strategic activities of the learner.

4. The strategic spirit has a high payoff in real-life settings, particularly as learners become adults. The long-term payoff makes this perhaps the most important reason. The strategic spirit helps people make thoughtful and intelligent decisions about such things as which job opportunities to pursue and where to live. Eventually, students will face the thinking challenges of life on their own, having to do such things as learn how to use a computer or a new computer program, fix a complex piece of machinery, solve a pressing problem at work, or deal with a delicate interpersonal matter. Having the strategic spirit gives people an advantage in situations like these because it counsels them to stand back, marshal their resources, make a plan, and deploy the plan intelligently.

It is also worth noting that in today's economy, the strategic spirit is increasingly valuable in the workplace. More and more frequently, workers today are being asked to make decisions on their own, to solve problems, to troubleshoot, and in general to be more independent, planful, and creative in their thinking. The consistent and creative use of these abilities is what having the strategic spirit is all about.

THE BOTTOM LINES: INCORPORATING THE STRATEGIC SPIRIT INTO THE CULTURE OF THE CLASSROOM

Here are four guidelines to help teachers cultivate in students a strategic and spirited attitude towards thinking challenges.

1. Provide models of the strategic spirit. Illustrate for students how people, including yourself, identify strategic opportunities in daily life and use thinking strategies to work through them.

2. Straightforwardly explain how to identify strategic moments, providing direct instruction in core strategy steps and their associated tactics. Explain to students in clear language the idea of the strategic spirit and why it is important and directly teach them the craft of inventing and using thinking strategies.

3. Provide opportunities for students to interact with you and each other around the use of thinking strategies. Engage students in discussions and activities where they are encouraged to use the language and tactics of strategic thinking in their interpersonal interactions.

4. Make sure there are feedback opportunities around the use of thinking strategies. Acknowledge and guide students' efforts to adopt the strategic spirit and arrange opportunities for students to give each other feedback about their use of thinking strategies.

Chapter 9 provides several practical examples of how to put these bottom lines to work in cultivating students' strategic spirit. In the pages that follow are illustrations of classroom practice, instructional guidelines, and specific tactics for enculturating the strategic spirit in students.

▶ 9

The Strategic Spirit: Pictures of Practice

Chapter 8 introduced the idea of the strategic spirit—a special kind of thinking disposition that takes the form of systematic, strategic thinking. Following the format of the previous "pictures of practice" chapters, this chapter provides several practical examples of how to cultivate students' strategic spirit as well as follow-up and troubleshooting ideas. Here is a preview of the sections to come:

1. **Strategy Building Blocks: Ms. Mandly and the Terrariums**
   This section explains how a teacher uses a build-a-strategy poster to teach students about core strategic building blocks, which they use to build a strategy to solve a problem in the classroom. (The build-a-strategy poster in this section is a resource that can be used in any classroom.)

2. **Build-a-Strategy across the Curriculum**
   Opportunities for thinking strategically in the subject matters abound— the trick is learning to see them. This section identifies diverse opportunities to build and use thinking strategies across the curriculum.

3. **Ready-Made: A Decision-Making Strategy**
   One of the more important thinking challenges we all face is the challenge of making wise and thoughtful decisions. This section presents a powerful decision-making strategy, along with suggestions about how students can use it to deepen understanding in different school subjects and to make important decisions in their own lives. While the decision-making strategy illustrated here is "ready-made," we show how it is constructed out of core strategy building blocks.

4. **Taking the Plunge: Guidelines for Instruction**
   A stepwise method of introducing the strategic spirit in your classroom teaching is offered.

5. **Continuing On: Making the Strategic Spirit a Permanent Part of the Classroom Culture**
   Suggestions for continuing to involve the strategic spirit in the classroom are laid out, organized by the four modes of enculturation—models, explanation, interaction, and feedback.

6. **Troubleshooting: Questions and Answers about the Strategic Spirit**
   This section identifies a few of the more frequently encountered obstacles in the use of thinking strategies and provides advice for teachers about how to deal with them.

STRATEGY BUILDING BLOCKS: MS. MANDLY AND THE TERRARIUMS

Ms. Mandly looks at the terrariums on the windowsill of her sixth-grade classroom and her heart sinks. What had begun as an exciting project now looked as if it might end in disaster. A month ago, working in groups of four, students had collected plant specimens in the woods behind the school and carefully planted them in gallon glass jugs. For the first week, students were thrilled about the project, and everyone seemed to want to take care of terrariums; there were even arguments among group members over who would get to water them. But lately terrarium care had grown inconsistent. No one was sure who was doing what, or who was responsible for what, and the terrariums were beginning to look ill. Whether it was due to overwatering, underwatering, or other factors entirely, nobody seemed to be sure. Ms. Mandly decides to take action, not just for the sake of the plants, but for the sake of her students.

On Ms. Mandly's classroom wall is a poster called build-a-strategy that identifies four basic thinking strategy steps (see Table 9.1 on page 107). The idea of the poster is that students can use one or more of the steps, in any order, to construct their own thinking strategies—strategies that they customize to suit the thinking challenge at hand. It took students a while to get the hang of using the poster, but now they see it as a part of regular classroom life. Ms. Mandly refers to the poster frequently when a thinking challenge arises in class, and she encourages students to refer to it, too, when they notice a thinking challenge on their own. Some of the thinking challenges students have identified include studying for a quiz, settling an argument, and understanding a difficult text. Today, Ms. Mandly hopes students will opt to use the strategy building blocks to deal with the problem of the terrariums.

TABLE 9.1   Build-a-Strategy

Strategy Building Blocks

When . . .	Strategy Step	Tactics
When you need to be clear about what you're doing or where you're going . . .	STATE . . . either the problem, the situation, or your goal(s).	Identify the different dimensions of the situation. Identify the parts of the situation you will focus on. State precisely what you want to change or what you want your outcome to be. Be specific!
When you need to think broadly about something . . .	SEARCH . . . for ideas, options, possibilities, purposes, features, assumptions, causes, effects, questions, dimensions, hypotheses, facts, or interpretations.	Brainstorm. Look for different kinds of ideas. Look at things from different points of view. Look for hidden ideas. Build on other people's ideas. Use categories to help you search.
When you need to assess, rate, or decide something . . .	EVALUATE . . . options, plans, ideas, theories, or objects	Look for lots of reasons. Consider the immediate and long-term consequences. List all the pros and cons, paying attention to both. Try to be objective; avoid bias. Use your imagination: how will it affect others?
When you need to think about the details of something . . .	ELABORATE . . . possibilities, plans, options, hypotheses, or ideas.	Make a detailed plan: Say what will happen at each step. Visualize what it will look/feel/ seem like *in detail*. Ask yourself: What resources will be used? How will it happen? Who will be affected? How long will it take? Think about the different parts. Draw a picture or write a description; imagine *telling* someone about it.

With this fond hope in mind, Ms. Mandly asks her students if they think the terrarium situation is a thinking challenge. After a moment of trying to pass the blame for the failing terrariums among each other, most students admit that it is. Time, asks Ms. Mandly, to use the strategy building blocks? Yes, it is.

Ms. Mandly: Let's take a look at the poster. How can we build a strategy to deal with this situation? Which building blocks can we use?

Rory: We should use the search step, to search for a solution to the problem.

Marc: Yeah, but we're not even exactly sure what the problem *is*. We don't know if the plants in the terrarium are wilted because they have too much water or too little.

Ms. Mandly: Are you suggesting we also need a state step, Marc?

Marc: (*After a moment of looking at the poster.*) Yes. In two ways: I think we need to state the problem *and* we need to state our goal.

Ms. Mandly: That sounds reasonable. Any other building blocks we can use?

The class is silent, and although Ms. Mandly is tempted to suggest that students also consider using the evaluate or elaborate steps, she refrains from saying anything . . . yet. On the board she writes:

> **STRATEGY FOR DEALING WITH**
> **THE TERRARIUM PROBLEM**
>
> Step 1. State the problem and goals
> Step 2. Search for possible solutions

Ms. Mandly: Now take a look at the *tactics* for the state step. We don't necessarily need to use all the tactics. What should we do?

Kim: Let's state what we want our outcome to be. We want to figure out who's supposed to take care of the terrarium, right?

Marc: Yeah, but that might not be enough. What if you take care of a terrarium, and it still wilts. Other people in your group will want to know what went wrong.

Ms. Mandly: It sounds like we have two goals here. One, decide how to care for the terrarium. And two, make a plan for keeping track of the terrarium's care.

After more discussion, students agree on exactly what outcomes they want, and move to step 2. Looking at the search tactics, they decide to brainstorm lots of different possible solutions. Ms. Mandly keeps track of their ideas on the blackboard, and occasionally reminds them to keep in mind some key tactics—to look for hidden ideas and to look for different kinds of ideas. Some of the ideas students come up with are:

1. have a sign-up list
2. let the teacher decide who should water
3. have one person volunteer to do it all
4. make a rotating scheduling for each group
5. make a rotating schedule, plus have weekly group meetings to discuss progress

After students review their brainstormed list, they unanimously agree that option 5—rotating schedule plus weekly meeting—is best. But then the discussion stalls. What next?

Ms. Mandly: Take a look at the poster. Are we through with our strategy now, or is there another step we could take?

Rory: Well, we have our idea, but now we have to figure out how it's going to get done. So maybe we should do the elaborate step.

Kim: I agree. But we don't need to use all the elaborate tactics, we just need to make a plan. *(Ms. Mandly changes the build-a-strategy on the blackboard to read the following.)*

STRATEGY FOR DEALING WITH THE TERRARIUM PROBLEM

Step 1. State the problem and goals
Step 2. Search for possible solutions
Step 3. Elaborate: Make a plan

The discussion continues. Students go on to design a rotation schedule for each terrarium group, and, with Ms. Mandly's help, they pick a time for weekly group meetings. Working through the elaborate step, they invent a detailed checklist for the designated weekly waterer, to help track factors that might contribute to the terrarium's health, such as how much water has been given, the date of watering, the temperature of classroom, and so on. After the groups have finished devising their plans, she pairs up groups and asks each group to critique another group's plan, noting what is good about it and what might need improvement.

While students are talking among themselves, Ms. Mandly walks over and inspects the terrariums on the windowsill. To be sure, several plant specimens are wilted, and some are dry and shriveled. But there is still vigor in a few sprouts. Ms. Mandly smiles to herself. Perhaps the terrariums may survive after all.

Meeting the Bottom Lines

In what ways does Ms. Mandly's lesson touch on the bottom lines mentioned in Chapter 8?

Bottom Line: Provide models of the strategic spirit. yes ☐ no ■

In the past, Ms. Mandly has modeled the strategic spirit for students by identifying, herself, strategic opportunities and showing how she uses the strategy building blocks to work through them. Today she simply encourages students to identify the strategic opportunity themselves.

Bottom Line: Straightforwardly explain how to identify strategic moments, providing direct instruction in core strategy steps and their associated tactics. yes ■ no ☐

Ms. Mandly refers to the building blocks poster and explains from time to time what to do. But her direct instruction is lean: In this activity, Ms. Mandly's main intention is to guide students to think for themselves.

Bottom Line: Provide opportunities for students to interact with you and each other about the use of thinking strategies. yes ■ no ☐

Through the use of careful questions, Ms. Mandly engages her students in verbally interacting with her and with each other as the class talks together about when and how to use the strategy building blocks. Equally importantly, following the class discussion she has students work in groups to devise plans for taking better care of the terrariums, thus encouraging student/student interaction around the strategic spirit without constant mediation by herself, the teacher.

Bottom Line: Make sure there are feedback opportunities about the use of thinking strategies. yes ■ no ☐

During the class discussion, Ms. Mandly acknowledges and guides students' efforts to adopt the strategic spirit, reinforcing their behavior at appropriate junctures (for instance, by commending Marc on his comment about goals). Also, by asking the groups to evaluate each others' plans at the close of the activity, Ms. Mandly creates an key opportunity for students to give and receive feedback from their peers.

Following Up: Integrating the Lesson into the Classroom Culture

Although at first Ms. Mandly had feared that she would overload her students by presenting the build-a-strategy to them, by now she knows that it was right to empower them with the building blocks to construct their own strategies. So she continues to model how to identify strategic opportunities and how to use the strategy building blocks. Over time, she needs to model less frequently because the students become able to build strategies quite well on their own. Occasionally, Ms. Mandley explains again how to use the building blocks when students are constructing a new strategy, but mostly she simply helps guide them. Primarily, she continues to structure strategy building around group interactions and provides opportunity for evaluation at the end so students receive feedback from one another. She herself also continues to reinforce and guide their efforts to embrace the strategic spirit.

BUILD-A-STRATEGY ACROSS THE CURRICULUM

Here are some examples of opportunities in the curriculum where strategies can be constructed out of the strategy building blocks on the build-a-strategy poster. For each of the following examples, first we identify the strategic opportunity, then we show a sample strategy that could be constructed to take advantage of the opportunity. For the first three examples, we also show what a teacher can actually say or do in the classroom to help students recognize the strategic moment.

As you are browsing these examples, notice how flexible the building blocks are. You can use them in any order whatsoever; you can use the same step repeatedly in the same strategy; and you can even create a strategy by simply using the same step more than once.

Strategic Opportunity: Studying for a quiz

Strategy

State your goal(s)
Search for different plans to meet your goal(s)
Evaluate the plans and choose a good one

Helping students recognize the strategic moment: Suggest to students that it makes sense to use a strategy to study for a quiz, then invite them to build their own strategy. Or, say something like: "Next week you'll be taking a quiz on the Mayan Indians. How will you study for it? Will you just plunge into studying, without a plan? What else could you do?"

Strategic Opportunity: Class discussion about why kids take drugs

Strategy

Search assumptions
Search causes
possibly go on to . . .
Search solutions to the problem of kids and drugs
Evaluate the most promising solutions
Elaborate on the best idea

Helping students recognize the strategic moment: As the discussion is beginning, say something like: "I hear a lot of opinions about this topic from you. Whenever there are lots of ideas around about a difficult issue, it helps to try to organize thinking. What could we do to organize our thinking around the issue of kids and drugs? What steps could we take to make sure that we capture everyone's ideas? Many of you have ideas about what *causes* kids to take drugs. So maybe we should brainstorm all the possible causes, to make sure we get a full view of the picture. It also seems that we all have many assumptions about drugs—assumptions about whether they are good or bad, who takes them, and so on. So perhaps we should also search for all our assumptions, and get them out in the open so we can understand the issue better. There. Now we have two steps we want to make sure to take. We want to search for causes, and search for assumptions. This is the beginning of a thinking strategy . . ."

Strategic Opportunity: Settling an argument in the classroom

Strategy

State the problem
Evaluate both sides
Search for an alternative solution

Helping students recognize the strategic moment: As things heat up, say something like: "Whoa . . . hold on. Do we want to keep arguing, or do we want to stand back and be strategic about this? What could we do to get clear about the issue? What steps could we take to hear all sides of the issue?" Or, straightforwardly ask students to stand back for a minute to build a strategy for settling the argument. Remind them of the core strategy building blocks.

Strategic Opportunity: Understanding a poem

Strategy

Search for possible interpretations
Evaluate the interpretations for interest and plausibility
Elaborate on those interpretation(s)

Strategic Opportunity: Learning how an ecosystem works

Strategy

Search for all the features of an ecosystem
Search for all the purposes an ecosystem serves
Evaluate how well an ecosystem works

Strategic Opportunity: Exploring the decision the Pilgrims faced, about whether to come to the "New World"

Strategy

State the decision point
Search for options
Evaluate the best options and decide what you would have done

As you can see, the strategy variations are almost as diverse as the opportunities to use them. What is important is cultivating in students the strategic *spirit*—the inclination to see regular classroom activities as opportunities to build, and use, thinking strategies similar to the ones listed above.

Because the foregoing example doesn't illustrate any particular classroom activity, it isn't useful to evaluate it in terms of the bottom lines. However, instruction around any of the strategic opportunities mentioned above can be shaped by any or all four cultural forces. Perhaps the most effective way to help students recognize strategic opportunities and build thinking strategies to meet them is to design instruction that combines the two cultural forces *models* and *explanation:* Model how to identify strategic opportunities in the classroom by doing so yourself, and straightforwardly explain how to construct strategies.

"READY-MADE": A DECISION-MAKING STRATEGY

In addition to self-built strategies, some strategies come ready-made. A ready-made strategy consists of a series of steps that is particularly effective in working through a frequently occurring thinking challenge. Decision making is such a challenge.

Making decisions plays an important role in many things we do. We decide how to spend our time, what to buy, what to believe, how to act. Decision making also plays an important role in schools subjects. For example, history is in large part a story of the decisions historical figures have made and their effects on others. The study of literature often involves appreciating why authors made the decisions they did in crafting works; and understanding a narrative work of literature often requires understanding why characters in the story make the choices they do. Because decision making is such a common thinking challenge, it is useful for students to have a powerful, ready-made decision-making strategy as part of their strategic repertoire. Here is a three-step strategy that can help students carefully think through decisions in their own lives, and in different subjects across the curriculum. The strategy is quite straightforward:

Decision-Making Strategy

Decision Point: Write out your question.

Step 1. Search for options

Step 2. Evaluate: list the complete reasons, pro and con, for the two or three most promising options

Step 3. Make a careful choice, supported by reasons

Steps 1 and 2 are familiar strategy building blocks, from the build-a-strategy poster. And, as usual, these steps are deepened by deploying their associated tactics. For example, step 1 is a search step, and the search tactics on the building block poster suggest brainstorming, looking for hidden ideas, and looking at things from different points of view. These tactics are useful when trying to go beyond the obvious either/or options of a decision point.

Here is an example of how the three-step decision-making strategy can be used to deepen students' thinking about a topic they are studying in school. Ms. Corriea's seventh-grade social studies class is studying a unit called "Labor in the United States." Students have recently read a chapter describing how children used to work in the mills of New England and how child labor laws have abolished that practice. As Ms. Corriea begins discussing the chapter, one student remarks that he wishes he could go to work. He says kids should be able to decide for themselves if they should work or go to school. Another student vehemently disagrees. "Twelve hours a day in the mills? No way!" A rather heated discussion starts, and Ms. Corriea suggests that students use a decision-making strategy to think through the issue.

"The law now states that children under the age of fourteen or sixteen, depending on the type of work and the hours, cannot hold jobs," Ms. Corriea explains. "Some people think child labor laws are necessary, because otherwise children will be taken advantage of, as they were in the mills. Other people say that child labor laws are unreasonable, and that working can be very educational for children, if it is carefully regulated. Let's not jump to conclusions about this; let's put on the strategic spirit and use a strategy to think through what decision we would recommend."

Ms. Corriea writes the decision-making strategy on the blackboard and fills in the decision point like this:

Decision Point: Should children be allowed to work?

Step 1. Search for options
Step 2. Evaluate: List the complete reasons, pro and con, for the two or three most promising options
Step 3. Make a careful choice, supported by reasons

Ms. Corriea explains the strategy to students. Experience has taught her that students are likely to have a little trouble going beyond the obvious options in step 1. So she does a little play-acting: "If I was doing step 1," she says, "I would ask myself what the obvious options are, and I would try to be imaginative about finding more options. For example, I might ask myself to think of the situation from different points of view. What options would kids think of? What options would employers think of? How about parents?"

Ms. Corriea divides students into groups of three and asks each group to use the strategy to make a decision. She circulates the classroom as the groups work, providing advice and support. Table 9.2 on page 116 shows what one group's thinking looked like.

When all the groups have made their choice, Ms. Corriea asks each group to report back to the rest of the class, explaining the reasons they made the choice they did. She concludes the lesson by asking students to reflect on how well they used the decision-making strategy: What went well with it? What parts were hard? How could they improve their use of the decision-making strategy next time?

Ms. Corriea uses this concluding discussion as an opportunity to provide her own feedback on what she noticed as she watched the groups work. For instance, she says that she noticed most people did indeed have a little trouble starting to brainstorm options. But when they stuck with it and did

continued on p. 117

TABLE 9.2 Decision Point: Should Children Be Allowed to Work?

OPTIONS

1. Allow children to work.
2. Don't allow children to work.
3. Let them work only after school.
4. Let them work where their parents work.
5. Let them work only at jobs that aren't unhealthy or dangerous.
6. Make working part of school.
7. Combine 3 and 5: Let kids work only after school, only a certain number of hours a week, and only at safe jobs.

COMPLETE REASONS
Promising Option #6: Make Work Part of School

Pros	Cons
1. Kids would make their own money, save their parents money.	1. Kids might not have enough time for classes or homework.
2. Work is a good way to learn about the real world.	2. Some kids already work at home, don't want to be forced to work as part of school.
3. School could make sure jobs were safe.	3. Kids could be taken advantage of.
	4. Kids might take work away from grown-ups who really need it.
	5. Might be an expensive program for the school to run.

Promising Option #7: Let Kids Work a Little, If It's Safe

Pros	Cons
1. It gives parents and kids a choice.	1. Kids might want to work but their parents won't let them.
2. It allows kids to work but not be harmed.	2. Even making laws won't make sure kids won't be hurt or taken advantage of.
3. It makes it so they can't be taken advantage of.	3. Kids might take jobs away from adults.
4. It won't cost the school anything.	4. They might not be able to find jobs they can do.
5. Kids will be making their own money.	

CAREFUL CHOICE

#7. Let kids work a little if it's safe, because the school-and-work option has too many really bad cons. This option gives people a choice. It has some cons, but they aren't as bad as the cons of other options, and the pros are very strong.

not give up, they generated some really interesting ideas. "Brainstorming is like that," she said. "It comes in waves."

Meeting the Bottom Lines

Ms. Corrica has taught a very extensive lesson on decision making, so not surprisingly, it coveres all four of the bottom lines.

Bottom Line: Provide models of the strategic spirit. yes ■ no ☐

Ms. Corriea uses her own thinking as a model for students, when she thinks aloud about how to go beyond the obvious options at step 1 of the strategy by looking at different points of view.

Bottom Line: Straightforwardly explain how to identify strategic moments, providing direct instruction in core strategy steps and their associated tactics. yes ■ no ☐

Students are directly alerted to the need for a decision-making strategy and Ms. Corriea provides one by writing it on the board. She also straightforwardly explains to students how to use the strategy before they begin working in groups.

Bottom Line: Provide opportunities for students to interact with you and each other using thinking strategies. yes ■ no ☐

Ms. Corriea makes sure students will interact with one another with the use of the decision-making strategy by asking students to work in groups of three. Working in groups will encourage students to use the language and adopt the spirit of thinking strategies with one another.

Bottom Line: Make sure there are feedback opportunities with the use of thinking strategies. yes ■ no ☐

By asking students to reflect on their use of the decision-making strategy after they have used it, Ms. Corriea creates an opportunity for students to provide self-feedback and give feedback to their peers. Knowing that it is important to provide feedback to students herself, she also makes constructive comments about students' thinking.

Following Up: Integrating the Lesson into the Classroom Culture

Ms. Corriea gives her students continued practice in using the decision-making strategy. She also devises other relevant ready-made strategies. For example, she draws on the build-a-strategy poster to construct a ready-made strategy for making an argument; she has students use it when debating sides in the social studies class. She makes a point of modeling each strategy herself in her own thinking. With the introduction of each new strategy, she explains in detail when and how to use it appropriately. Students usually work in groups so they have opportunity to interact. Ms. Corriea continues to set up many opportunities for students to give themselves and each other feedback, and provides abundant feedback herself as well.

TAKING THE PLUNGE: GUIDELINES FOR INSTRUCTION

If you have found the idea of the strategic spirit appealing, by all means try teaching it to your students. As usual, we recommend plunging into instruction even if you may feel slightly shaky about exactly what to do (remember Michelangelo!).

You may have a personal plan that makes special sense for your situation. Alternatively, here is a series of steps that can help you introduce the strategic spirit to your class. Although in other "pictures of practice" chapters we have usually provided two plunge points, this time we offer just one because it is a generic way to introduce the strategy building blocks.

Plunge Point

1. Choose a thinking challenge around which to build a lesson (see the previous "Build-a-Strategy across the Curriculum" example for sample strategic opportunities).

2. Plan a time to introduce the build-a-strategy poster and to guide students in its use.

3. Reread the example, Ms. Mandly's terrarium. Using Ms. Mandly's approach as a guide, decide how you will explain the strategic spirit and the building block poster to students, and what aspects of it you will model. Make sure that you straightforwardly explain the idea of the strategic spirit, and make sure that the poster is visually accessible to students.

4. Explain each building block, drawing students' attention to the tactics associated with each one.

5. Ask students to use the strategy building blocks to design a strategy to deal with the thinking challenge you have identified.

6. Consider whether you want students to interact together at this point using a thinking strategy. If so, design an activity that involves students talking and planning together. For example, you might build the strategy as a whole class and do the first step together, then ask students to work in pairs to do the remainder of the steps.

7. Make sure to give students feedback about their use of the strategy building blocks, not only at the end of the activity, but also as the activity proceeds. You may also want to consider ways to have students provide feedback to each other.

8. Congratulate yourself. You have started helping your students develop the strategic spirit!

CONTINUING ON: MAKING THE STRATEGIC SPIRIT A PERMANENT PART OF THE CLASSROOM CULTURE

After you introduce your students to the strategic spirit and the strategy building blocks, there are many ways to continue to build the strategic spirit into the culture of your classroom. Here are some ideas, organized according to the four cultural forces.

Models of the Strategic Spirit

- Model the strategic spirit yourself. When you engage in decision making, planning, making an argument, solving a problem, or other strategic situations, often take the opportunity to model the strategic spirit for your students. Illustrate, and at times explicitly elucidate, how you employ state, search, evaluate, and elaborate steps, as appropriate, during your thinking process.
- Direct students' attention to examples of the strategic spirit. Illustrate for students how people, including yourself, identify strategic opportunities in daily life. Identify candidate situations for the use of strategy building blocks. Remember, the strategic spirit involves *seeking* strategic opportunities, as well as working through them. So, when approaching a thinking situation, model the strategic spirit by asking students, "Should we be building a strategy here?"

Explanations of the Strategic Spirit

- Straightforwardly explain to students the purpose of the strategic spirit. Make it clear that the strategic spirit means not just knowing sets of specific strategies but also approaching situations in a strategic way. It means recognizing occasions that invite strategic thinking and constructing tactics appropriate to the new situation.

- Straightforwardly explain the purpose of each strategy building block and how it helps to make thinking better. Refer to the "when" category in the build-a-strategy poster for ideas about the purposes of the building blocks.
- Provide direct instruction in when and how to use thinking strategies. Help students identify occasions by first explaining when one can productively use strategies. Then, as thinking situations arise, ask students if the situation at hand is an occasion that would benefit from the use of thinking strategies. Give students ample practice in using the steps of the strategy building blocks. Refer to the exercises in this chapter for suggestions.
- Keep visual reminders of strategic thinking prominently displayed in the classroom. Hang the build-a-strategy poster, or your own version of it, for reference during lessons and for students to use as guidance in their own work. On written assignments and comments, put visible reminders for students to be strategic in their thinking.

Interactions Involving the Strategic Spirit

- Use the language of the strategic spirit when talking with students and encourage them to use it with you and with each other. Habitually use the terms *state, search, evaluate,* and *elaborate* when building a strategy and insist that students use them to structure their strategy building.
- Engage students in cooperative activities using the thinking strategies. When there are thinking challenges, allow for discussion and interpersonal interaction. Let students work together in generating tactics of strategic thinking so they can construct strategies together as well as give mutual support and feedback.

Feedback about Strategic Thinking

- Let students know what their strengths and weakness are regarding strategic thinking. Acknowledge and reinforce students' efforts to adopt the strategic spirit. When they neglect strategic opportunities or falter in their efforts to use strategies, guide and support them in building strategic attitudes and tactics.
- Provide opportunities for students to give each other feedback about their use of thinking strategies. Allow time for students to give each other feedback in classroom work and in cooperative activities.
- Encourage self-feedback. Build in reflection time following thinking challenges so that students have the opportunity to think about what worked and what did not work in their use of thinking strategies.

- Try to make all feedback informative and learning centered. Encourage a mutually supportive, rather than judgmental, environment in which anyone can offer worthwhile feedback.

Checking Your Progress

A weekly chart completed at the week's end can help you to see your progress. It covers the four modes of enculturation: models, explanation, interaction, and feedback. Table 9.3 on page 122 is a sample chart filled out with some possible thinking activities a teacher might do during the week. In this sample situation, the teacher has already introduced the build-a-strategy poster to the students the previous month; during this week, the teacher wants them to practice building strategies in new situations.

TROUBLESHOOTING: QUESTIONS AND ANSWERS ABOUT THE STRATEGIC SPIRIT

It takes quite a bit of classroom time to have students build and use a thinking strategy, even if it's only a two-step strategy. Won't teaching thinking strategies take time away from teaching content?

While it's true that using thinking strategies takes time, it is important to remember that the kinds of strategies we talk about in this chapter *enhance* content learning. For instance, examples were given of how a decision-making strategy can deepen students' thinking about historical and literary decision points covered in the curriculum. In another example, the build-a-strategy building blocks were used to construct strategies to help students study, to help them understand difficult concepts, and to tackle other content-related challenges.

Through a little advance planning, you can cultivate students' strategic spirit, *and* ensure that the curriculum is covered. Do this by looking over upcoming lessons and identifying opportunities that invite deep thinking. Ask yourself: Where are difficult concepts? Where are the problems to be solved? Where are the places students might think impulsively or perseverate fruitlessly along a single thinking track? As you are teaching, help students to be alert to these moments, and guide them to construct strategies around them.

Sure, it's a nice idea to get students to notice thinking challenges on their own so that they can use thinking strategies to deal with them. But let's face it—my students rarely do *anything* on their own. They wait for me to tell them what to do. So how do I get them to notice thinking challenges?

TABLE 9.3 The Strategic Spirit Weekly Chart

	MONDAY	TUESDAY	WEDNESDAY	THURSDAY	FRIDAY
Models		Resuming computer discussion, I modeled a little bit of strategic thinking.		We reviewed choices colonists made that led to Boston Tea Party.	
Explanation	The build-a-strategy poster is on the wall. We decided how to share and maintain our new computer. Had several discussions but no conclusive answer.	I reminded students that we should approach this strategically. I review the STATE goals, SEARCH and EVALUATE steps.		We talk about the options they had, and what the tradeoffs were. I relate this to the SEARCH and EVALUATE strategies.	I give an assignment to write an essay and instructed students to use the strategies in deciding on a topic.
Interaction		We set up group committees for: sharing time, security, maintenance. Students used the strategies to come up with proposed plans.	The committees reported on their plans, and I had them talk about the tactics they used to arrive at the plans.	I had students search for, elaborate, and evaluate other options the colonists might have had. They discussed among themselves.	
Feedback			Students gave feedback, e.g., some groups needed more options. I gave my feedback too.	Students and I give each other feedback on the process.	

122

Often, traditional education doesn't encourage students to take the initiative in learning situations. So it's not all that surprising that they wait to be told what to do. This is what they believe is expected of them. To change things, change students' expectations. Show them that you expect them to be aware of the thinking challenges around them.

One way to do this is to straightforwardly ask students to keep a notebook in which they record the times each day when they find themselves thinking hard about something, when they find themselves feeling confused or puzzled, and when they find themselves with a problem to solve or decision to make. (If you do an activity like this, it helps to give quotas. For example, tell students to identify at least three thinking challenges a day. It's often a lot easier for students to fill a specified quota than to guess about your expectations.) Soon, students will have a notebook full of thinking challenges that they themselves have identified, around which you can guide them to construct thinking strategies.

Another way to encourage students to notice thinking challenges is to model how you notice your own thinking challenges, and how you think strategically about them. For example, think aloud when you have to make a decision. Show yourself identifying the decision point and model how you construct a strategy to deal with it. Or think aloud when you encounter a difficult concept. For example, show yourself recognizing the thinking challenge of understanding how photosynthesis works, and model how you strategically step back and plan what steps to take to try to understand the process more deeply.

Many of my classroom materials include things called strategies, but they aren't like the strategies you talk about here. For example, I have materials that teach a reading comprehension strategy, a spelling strategy, and so on. What is the relationship between these kinds of strategies and the ones you are talking about?

The strategies we talk about in this chapter involve broad creative and critical thinking steps—steps where you have to think independently and where there is no single right answer. Sometimes, things that go by the name of thinking strategies have a more limited purpose. They tell you exactly what to do, because there is a very good specific way to tackle the task at hand. For example, a reading strategy might include steps that tell you to (1) read all the topic headings in the chapter, then (2) write down all the words you don't understand. Advice like this is very direct. It can address a particular need in a valuable way, but it doesn't make room for individual choice or variation.

Recipe-like strategies can be very useful in the same way that a recipe for making tapioca can be very useful when tapioca is exactly what you want to make. But cultivating the strategic spirit means encouraging students to use their own critical judgment about deciding which strategy steps to take, and how to take them. If you have classroom materials that include things labeled *strategies*, take a close look at them. Make sure that at least some of the strategies you teach include broad creative and critical thinking steps like the ones described on the build-a-strategy poster, so that your students have opportunities to identify and make strategic decisions on their own.

10

Higher Order
Knowledge

*Higher Order Knowledge: 1. The knowledge and craft
of solving problems and managing tasks in a discipline.
2. The knowledge and craft of evidence and explanation in
a discipline. 3. The knowledge and craft of discovery and
invention in the discipline.*

How do you play the science game? Count Rumford had some ideas about
that. Count Rumford displayed the pattern of scientific thinking about as
elegantly and clearly as anyone could wish.

During the latter half of the eighteenth century, a battle raged in the
scientific community about the nature of heat. The favored theory held
that heat consisted of a kind of substance called *caloric*. Certain processes,
such as burning or friction, drove this caloric out of a substance, making it
detectable.

While many scientists championed the caloric theory of heat, others
harbored skepticism. One of these was Count Rumford, who suspected that
heat was another kind of thing altogether. But how could Count Rumford
test whether there really was a substance called caloric?

To test the caloric theory, Count Rumford turned to an odd manifesta-
tion of friction: The boring of cannons. A cannon was made by casting a solid
piece of metal in the shape of a cannon, then boring a hole in it to accept the
powder and cannon ball. The boring of the cannon of course generated
enormous heat. According to the caloric theory, this occurred because the
friction of the bit drove the caloric out of the cannon.

Count Rumford asked a simple and elegant question: If caloric is a substance, there can only be so much of it in the cannon in the first place. So what would happen if we *kept* boring the cannon for a long time? Count Rumford arranged an experiment with a dull bit, where one could keep boring a cannon without breaking through the back of it. The boring continued for days. But no matter how long the process proceeded, the cannon still gave off enormous heat. Count Rumford's conclusion: The caloric theory had to be wrong, because, if it were right, the cannon would run out of caloric and stop giving off heat.

Count Rumford's experiment, a classic in physics, shows us something about how science works as an area of inquiry. We see in Rumford's investigation the basic pattern of hypothetico-deductive reasoning. The hypothesis was a theory, the caloric model of heat. The deduction was the prediction that friction eventually would drive all the caloric out of something; with no caloric left, friction would no longer heat it. Rumford set up a test of this prediction and found it wanting.

It is easy to generalize from this science example to other disciplines. For example, history has its own patterns for testing claims and investigating situations. While experiments provide the key evidence in science, original sources provide the key evidence in history. While science involves creating theories or models, history involves constructing interpretations of events that help us to understand why a particular historical episode happened as it did.

If different disciplines have different ways of testing truth, pursuing inquiries, and solving problems, how does education deal with this? By and large, by ignoring it. Instruction generally does not delve into how a discipline actually works. True, students of science sometimes study the "scientific method," maybe even learning about the Rumford example. But they only study it as more information. They do not really engage in scientific thinking and develop a feel for the enterprise. Similarly, students of history typically learn little about how history works—how historians establish facts and reach interpretations.

Hence, there are aspects of a discipline that are more general than conventional content and routine skills and that concern how one engages in the discipline. We will call these aspects "higher order knowledge." They are "higher order" because they sit above the regular content knowledge in a discipline. Students cannot really understand school subject matter without understanding the higher order aspects.

Imagine, for example, Mr. Wing's dilemma when he begins to think more carefully about the science experiment concerning plant growth in which he usually engages his fifth-grade class. The experiment goes like this. Mr. Wing provides pots, soil, and bean seeds. The experiment concerns the impact of sunlight on plant growth. The students place some plants in the window, some in the closet. They graph the plants' growth over the next several weeks, looking for the impact of the sunlight.

The trouble is, Mr. Wing says to himself, *the kids already know what's going to happen. It's not a real experiment. It's going through the motions. And it doesn't really give kids any idea what science is all about.*

Mr. Wing pauses to ponder how he can remake the experiment so that it more authentically represents a process of scientific inquiry. "One thing for sure," he says to himself, "if this is going to be anything like real science, the hypotheses have to come from my students. And they can't all be as obvious as plants responding to sunlight."

After some careful planning, he involves his fifth graders in quite a different form of the plant experiment. He begins by writing "Plant Growth" in big letters on the blackboard. "What do you think might effect plant growth?" he asks his students. "What might matter—anything at all. Let's do a serious brainstorm around this. I want a big list."

His students oblige. Resolved to be open about the possibilities students suggest, Mr. Wing puts down even oddball hypotheses. Here are some of the proposals the students make:

- amount of sunlight
- length of the day
- how much water they get
- how deep a seed is to start with
- fertilizer
- how often they get watered, not just how much
- the kind of light, like light bulbs versus daylight
- the kind of soil
- whether you grow them in sand or leaves or whatever
- fresh air
- talking to them, touching them
- closeness to other plants of the same kind
- warmth
- moist air, not just watering

Mr. Wing then divides his class up into small groups of four students. Each group has to choose a hypothesis that looks promising to them. They need to write out *why* they think that this factor might make a difference. Then they need to figure out a way to test it.

Mr. Wing insists on a further twist. "One thing," he says to the class. "No picking a factor you already know the answer to. Nothing right out of the book. For instance, we all know that plants respond to light. So nothing like 'one pot in the window, one pot in the closet.' "

One student has an objection. "But we don't know *everything* about light. Like what about daylight versus light bulbs. Or can a plant tell there's light up there before the seed breaks through the surface."

"Okay," says Mr. Wing. "Anything we don't know, where you can spell out a reason why it might be plausible, you can test that."

Soon, he finds that his students have invested themselves much more thoroughly in their projects than with the typical windowsill-closet plant experiment. They "own" the ideas they seek to test. They have a fairly free hand (with Mr. Wing's counsel) in inventing how to test them. Mr. Wing takes care to coach the students about control of variables—ensuring that the key variable they are testing is the only contrast between the situations that they set up. Soon, a little scientific community is thriving within the four walls of Mr. Wing's classroom.

WHAT IS HIGHER ORDER KNOWLEDGE?

The general idea of higher order knowledge is simple: Any discipline consists of more than just facts and skills. Mathematics, for instance, is made up of more than the algorithms for addition, subtraction, multiplication, and division, indeed more than the Pythagorean theorem or the quadratic formula. Understanding literature involves more than having read Shakespeare and Frost, more than being able to recall some powerful features of their writing and some interpretations of their message.

But what is this "more"? There are many ways of articulating the nature of higher order knowledge. Recently, David Perkins and Rebecca Simmons offered a scheme that distinguishes three levels of higher order knowledge in a discipline, beyond the familiar "content" level (Perkins & Simmons, 1988).

Problem-Solving Level

Here we find knowledge and know-how about handling typical problems and tasks in the discipline. For example, what strategies can students use to tackle mathematics problems effectively, or to face the problem of organizing an essay in English or history? How do they go about finding topics worth writing about, when they have an essay assignment where they choose their own topic?

Evidence Level

The evidence level of knowledge concerns knowledge and know-how about evidence and explanation in a discipline. Every discipline has characteristic ways of justifying and explaining things. For example, the canons of evidence in mathematics and the sciences are quite different from one another. In mathematics, we want logical deductive proof of claims. The classic example is Euclidean geometry, where all theorems derive by deductive logic from the assumed axioms and definitions. In science, evidence takes quite another form. As illustrated by the Count Rumford example, we create models or theories and test their predictions to validate the models or theories. In literature, the form of evidence takes on yet another shape. To validate a generalization or interpretation about a work of literature, you need to look to the text, seeking evidence in what happens and how the author expresses it.

Inquiry Level

The inquiry level of knowledge and know-how concerns how inquiry proceeds in a discipline. What is it like to *do* history, for instance? What are good questions like? How does one go about pursuing them? History emphasizes the effort to reconstruct events and the interpretation of causes and trends. Literary inquiry involves cultivating sensitive response to works and probing them for their meanings and resonances. Science involves finding phenomena of interest, formulating questions worth asking, and constructing theories with explanatory power. As these points suggest, the inquiry level draws on the evidence level. But the inquiry level goes beyond matters of justification and explanation to include searching for questions and constructing themes and theories.

How distinct are the problem-solving, evidence, and inquiry levels? Inevitably, rich episodes of thinking in a discipline blend them together. It's not terribly important to classify a particular teaching episode into one or the other definitively. But the notion of higher order knowledge sounds a call to expand instruction to a fuller range, encompassing not only content knowledge but knowledge and know-how about problem solving, evidence, and inquiry.

WHY IS HIGHER ORDER KNOWLEDGE IMPORTANT?

In our reach toward a culture of thinking in schools, higher order knowledge of the disciplines has great importance for three principal reasons.

1. Higher order knowledge has not received adequate attention in conventional instruction. Most instruction occurs at the "content" level, focusing on the facts, algorithms, and skills of the discipline in question. Thus, the study of history highlights the textbook's story of what happened when and why. It rarely deals with the nature of historical evidence or the process of historical inquiry. Instruction in science typically dwells on the findings of science rather than the method. When scientific method receives some attention, it often takes a superficial form, the dilemma that troubled Mr. Wing in the opening example. As in his case, students may go through the motions of doing experiments in the name of learning how science is done. But "canned" experiments with outcomes that everyone knows in advance constitutes a very unauthentic experience of science.

The one concession to higher order knowledge in conventional education is plenty of problem solving in certain subject matters—science and mathematics, for instance. But even this concession has severe limits. While students receive abundant practice, they rarely are provided with any direct instruction in the craft of problem solving. They simply are asked to tackle large numbers of problems. In English, the analog of problem solving is the writing assignment. Here again, students commonly receive frequent writing assignments but very little direct instruction in the craft of writing, beyond mechanics.

2. Higher order knowledge holds keys to a genuine understanding of and involvement in a discipline. Higher order knowledge is supremely important to genuine understanding of and involvement in a discipline. For example, to know some science content but little about how science is done is to have a very limited and blinkered understanding of the scientific enterprise. To know a few stock interpretations of poems and plays but not know how one arrives at personal readings is to have an impoverished grasp of what it is to read literature with appreciation and insight. The same argument can be repeated for other disciplines. Students without a higher order perspective are likely to think of the disciplines simply as bundles of facts and skills. Somebody out there (adults, teachers, experts) knows the answers and the students are supposed to learn them.

But often students cannot really understand the facts, algorithms, and skills of a discipline without higher order knowledge. For example, many key ideas in science seem quite counterintuitive to the novice. A well-known case in point is the notion that objects, "left to themselves," continue at the same speed in the same direction, one of Newton's laws. Our experience of the world suggests quite the contrary: Objects slow down and come to a halt when left to themselves. Although Newton's laws fly in the face of our ordinary experience of everyday objects, they have an advantage: They offer better predictions and explanations about the way the world in general behaves, everything from the trajectory of a baseball to the orbits of the planets. To appreciate this, students need to gain a sense of the enterprise of science—how science reaches for universal laws that often cut beneath the obvious phenomena and require us to see them in a new way.

3. Students commonly have higher order misconceptions about disciplines that pose barriers to their progress. Attention to higher order knowledge is important because students already have ideas about it—and the ideas often lead them in unfortunate directions. In mathematics, for example, students commonly express the view that "if you can't solve it in ten minutes, you can't solve it at all" (Schoenfeld, 1985). Notice that this precept addresses no particular aspect of mathematics. It is a higher order premise, about mathematical problem solving in general, indeed part of what we called the "problem-solving level." Such a premise constitutes part of what we might call students' "background beliefs" about mathematics. Those background beliefs make a big difference in how students invest themselves in the study of mathematics. Most obviously, a student who subscribes to the "ten-minute rule" is likely to work for a few minutes on a problem and then simply give up. Such a student believes that you cannot unlock a problem by persistence, comparison with other problems, breaking the problem into components, looking at special cases, and so on. "You either get it or you don't."

In an area as remote from mathematics as writing, students also display views of the enterprise that powerfully shape their behavior. The researchers Carl Bereiter and Marlene Scardamalia have written about the "knowledge telling" strategy that many students use to manage writing tasks. Many students are quite frank about the strategy, saying something more or less like this:

> *I think of something I know to say about the topic. Then I write it down. Then I think of something else to say. And so on. Pretty soon I have a few paragraphs. When I run out of things to say, then I round it out with some kind of ending, and I'm done.*

Bereiter and Scardamalia underscore how starkly such a writing strategy contrasts with the working patterns of more seasoned writers. As the craft of writing develops, students become "knowledge transformers" rather than "knowledge tellers." Rather than just telling what they know, they think about it, rework it, identify claims, develop arguments, articulate personal perspectives, and so on (Bereiter & Scardamalia, 1985).

In summary, these examples from mathematics and writing show how fundamental the learner's overall conception of the discipline is to a learner's behavior. More attention to higher order knowledge in diverse ways becomes a key to students' enlightened learning.

THE BOTTOM LINES: INCORPORATING HIGHER ORDER KNOWLEDGE INTO THE CULTURE OF THE CLASSROOM

The foregoing discussion paints a broad picture of higher order knowledge in a discipline. But what does it mean to build into instruction day by day and week by week more attention to higher order knowledge? As a teacher, how can you tell whether you are doing this? Here are four "bottom line" principles to help gauge your progress toward developing students' higher order knowledge of the disciplines.

1. Model higher order knowledge using real-world examples. Provide examples of how problem solving, evidence, and inquiry work with real-world examples—actual scientific discoveries, historical research, substantive literary works, and so on. Remember, small-scale personal and accessible examples can often serve as well as grand episodes from the history of the disciplines.

2. Provide explanation of higher order knowledge within disciplines. Several times during a course of instruction, directly discuss with students how problem solving, explanation and the giving of evidence, and inquiry work in the discipline being taught.

In addition, you might make comparisons across disciplines. Discuss with the students contrasts between this and other disciplines in terms of how to solve problems, explain ideas, give evidence, and make discoveries.

3. Encourage interaction. Frequently engage students in activities of problem solving, explanation and evidence giving, or inquiry, where they also reflect on and articulate what they are doing and why in interaction with you and with one another. Draw from students their own conceptions of how to solve problems, explain and give evidence, and inquire in the discipline, and encourage students to discuss their conceptions with one another.

4. Be sure students get feedback around higher order knowledge. Give students positive feedback when they demonstrate understanding and appropriate use of higher order knowledge relevant to the discipline. When students display weak understanding of the higher order knowledge concepts, correct and reinforce the concepts through continued explanation. Through group work and other means, put students in situations where they will give one another feedback concerning higher order aspects of the subject matters as part of working through activities.

In Chapter 11 several classroom examples of teaching higher order knowledge, instructional guidelines, and tactics for keeping higher order knowledge alive in the culture of the classroom are provided.

▶ 11

Higher Order Knowledge: Pictures of Practice

This chapter looks at the practical side of higher order knowledge: How do you teach it? Where do you start? How can it become an ongoing part of the classroom culture? The pages that follow aim to answer all of these questions. Here is a preview of the upcoming sections:

1. **Lexington Green**
   Conventional instruction in history focuses on the story of "what happened" with little attention to how historians reach the conclusions that they do. This activity awakens students to the dilemmas of interpreting the historical record.

2. **Anchoring Analogies**
   Many students find the key concepts in physics do not make intuitive sense. The method of "anchoring analogies" plays students' intuitions about different situations against one another to build awareness of the importance of a consistent view of phenomena in a physical theory.

3. **Trash Anthropology**
   Many of the civilizations of the past left no written records and speak to us only through the artifacts that survive. This lesson helps students to understand the interpretive challenges of reconstructing ways of life in the distant past.

4. **Pair Problem Solving**
   Many students do not manage well the process of solving word problems in mathematics. By thinking together in pairs, with specific assigned roles, students can learn the ins and outs of the craft of problem solving.

5. **What Frost Meant**
   Robert Frost's "Stopping by the Woods on a Snowy Evening" becomes the occasion for exploring how evidence for an interpretation might be sought in English, in history, and in science, comparing the forms of evidence in the three disciplines.

6. **Taking the Plunge: Guidelines for Instruction**
   Two different starting points for beginning to include higher order knowledge in the teaching of disciplines, each with step-by-step guidelines.

7. **Continuing On: Making Higher Order Knowledge a Permanent Part of the Classroom Culture**
   Tips and strategies for incorporating higher order knowledge into the classroom culture.

8. **Troubleshooting: Questions and Answers about Higher Order Knowledge**
   Common concerns and what to do about them.

LEXINGTON GREEN

On April 19, 1775, the "shot heard 'round the world," reputedly the first shot of the American Revolution, was fired in Lexington, Massachusetts. While the events of that pivotal day stand out clearly in outline, historians are vexed by a subtle point of history. Who fired that first shot, or indeed whether the person was a colonial or British soldier, remains something of a mystery.

A number of years ago, Peter Bennett constructed an instructional unit called "What Happened at Lexington Green?" that simultaneously acquaints students with some of the events that launched the revolutionary war and exposes them to the dilemmas of historical reasoning. Bennett's curriculum unit also can be taken as a model for similar activities that plunge students into the midst of the complexities and ambiguities of historical evidence (Bennett, 1970).

"What Happened at Lexington Green?" brings original source materials to students for their examination. Early in the unit, the students review various testimonials regarding the first shot, some from colonists and some from the British. They analyze the trends in the comments. They ponder the weight of the evidence, which appears emphatically mixed.

As the students progress through the unit, they receive further information of the sort important to a historian. They learn something of the circumstances under which the eyewitness testimonies occurred. Some surprises are in store for them. At one point, a dialog something like this might occur between Peter Bennett (or any teacher) and the students:

Bennett: So what do you think now about this testimony?

Student: It looked pretty good at first.

Bennett: You changed your mind?

Student: Well, when we look at this further information, we find out that this guy told his story fifty years after it all happened.

Bennett: So what's wrong with that?

Student: People don't always remember so well.

Bennett: Any other problems with any of these accounts?

Student: Yeah, this guy from the British army who said that the British fired the first shot. That looked pretty good in the first place.

Bennett: Why did it look pretty good?

Student: Well, the guy seemed to be testifying against his own interest, you know. And when people testify against their own interests, you're more likely to trust them.

Bennett: So what went wrong? Why are you more skeptical now.

Student: It says here that when the guy said these things, he was a captive of the American forces. Well, it sure isn't in his interest to say how they started the war.

With the diverse evidence and its circumstances before them, students can make their best conclusion about who fired the first shot. But the fact of the matter is that the evidence remains vexed, for the students and even for historians. The real payoff of the experience lies not in determining who actually fired the first shot, but in learning about some of the bedevilments of historical evidence.

Bennett: What does this experience tell us about history? How do we know what happened two hundred years ago?

Student: We can't really *know.*

Bennett: Can we be pretty sure?

Student: Sometimes we can. Sometimes there's lots of evidence.

Bennett: And other times?

Student: Sometimes there's hardly any. Or a kind of mix. And it's messy. You have to figure out what's likely and maybe more than one thing looks reasonable.

Bennett: What does this tell you about what historians have to do?

Through discussions such as these, students can be led to recognize that history is the product of elaborate reconstruction by historians, often in the face of troubling ambiguity.

Meeting the Bottom Lines

Mr. Bennett touches on only two of the bottom lines for teaching higher order knowledge mentioned in the previous chapter, but he does so in a powerful way.

Bottom Line: Use real-world examples to model higher order knowledge in a discipline. yes ■ no ☐

"What Happened at Lexington Green" is a real world example of historical investigation that historians have struggled over. Thus, it is a model of the seeking of higher order knowledge. Since it involves actual events, it engages students in the complexities of historical reasoning and use of evidence. It also provides the teacher with a rich framework for discussing higher order knowledge.

Bottom Line: Provide explanation of higher order knowledge within a discipline. yes ☐ no ■

Mr. Bennett does not offer direct explanations of how inquiry or justification work in history in this episode. He is more interested in giving his students an initial experience of the dilemmas and drawing some preliminary insights from them. Following these early discussions, he can then begin to explicitly discuss and explain the nature of historical evidence and inquiry.

Bottom Line: Encourage interaction. yes ■ no ☐

Through his dialog with students, Mr. Bennett creates an arena for interactive, reflective examination of the nature of history. The lesson does not specifically tie in students' conceptions or encourage student/student interaction, but Mr. Bennett does build this into his follow-up lessons.

Bottom Line: Be sure that students receive feedback for higher order knowledge. yes ☐ no ■

This is an introductory lesson, so feedback comes later. In follow-up lessons, Mr. Bennett gives feedback to bolster students' understanding of the nature of historical inquiry.

Following Up: Integrating the Lesson into the Classroom Culture

Mr. Bennett has several ideas for continuing to build higher order knowledge about history in his students. He will bring in more real examples of historical events for his students to investigate and explicitly discuss with them how the process of inquiry and demands for evidence are similar across different cases. He will have them talk about their conceptions of history and what historians do and contrast it with their experiences during the exercises in these lessons. He will create expectations by calling on students to ask a good historical question or justify a position and by highlighting such themes in written assignments. This will provide occasions to offer students feedback and to set up sessions where they give feedback to one another as part of small-group discussion.

ANCHORING ANALOGIES

Suppose you put a book on a table. Clearly, the book pushes down on the table. But does the table push up on the book?

Ms. Mary Fulton's students mostly answer no. The table is too rigid to push back, they say. Unfortunately, Newton's laws say just the opposite. Newton's laws recognize that in a static situations such as the book resting on the table, forces must stand in balance with one another. The book cannot push down on the table without the table pushing up on the book. This principle helps Newton's laws to express a coherent and powerful view of the behavior of the physical world. But it remains puzzling to students, who cannot so readily appreciate the orderly and consistent treatment of physical reality inherent in the Newtonian viewpoint.

Researcher John Clement and his colleagues at the University of Massachusetts, Amherst, have searched for ways to help high school students understand this and other puzzling concepts from physics. One of the powerful tactics they have investigated in classroom settings involves the use of what they call "anchoring analogies." (Clement, 1982). An anchoring analogy is a special case that makes the phenomenon in question clear. Other more puzzling cases can be analyzed by comparison with the anchoring analogy.

What does this mean in the case of the book on the table? Imagine a dialog something like this between Ms. Fulton and a group of students.

Ms. Fulton: So you don't think that the table pushes back on the book.

Students: No.

Ms. Fulton: Okay. But let me ask you about another case. Imagine a book set on top of a big spring. Now does the spring push back on the book, or not?

Students: Sure.

Ms. Fulton: How come the spring pushes back but the table doesn't?

Student: Well, the spring compresses. It's springy. You could even see it compress if we really did it.

Ms. Fulton: Okay, that makes sense. But what about the table.

Student: The book doesn't bend the table. Tables aren't like springs. They're stiff.

Ms. Fulton: Well, maybe they are. Let's take another case. Let's imagine a very thin table, with a very bendy top. What happens when you put the book on it?

Student: The table bends down a little bit. And so I guess it pushes back on the book.

Continuing the dialog, the teacher leads the student to recognize a dilemma. If we start with a thin table and imagine thicker and thicker tables, it seems arbitrary to say that at a certain point the table stops bending at all. Finally, some students say, "Probably the regular table bends a little bit and pushes back on the book."

Of course, not all students will find such a sequence of arguments persuasive. The artful teacher can get out of the loop and engage them in arguing with one another about the logic of the matter. If the students too easily come to the conclusion that the table pushes back on the book, the teacher can up the ante with an even more intuitively puzzling case: "Now imagine a fly. A fly lands on the table. The fly weighs only a little bit. The fly pushes down on the table. But does the table push up on the fly?"

With enough arguing back and forth, puzzling over extreme cases and intermediate cases, many students come to the conclusion that the table always pushes back—and by just the same amount as the book or even the fly pushes down.

Finally, the discourse presents an opportunity to invite students into a confrontation with their ideas about what physics should be like. "So," the teacher might ask, "we've pretty much decided that our original intuitions are off base. The book seems too light initially for the table to push back, and the fly much too light for the table to push back. But, in the end, it makes sense to say that the table pushes back in both cases. What do we say about our original intuitions? Why have we decided they don't hold up? How far can we trust them? How do we test them? What makes us willing to give them up in this case?"

Discussion of these questions provides a natural ramp into an even more general question: "What does all this tell us about doing science?" With some help from the teacher, students can come to see that a broad principle of unity comes into play here. A neater picture of the world results if one says that the table always pushes back to match the weight on it, no matter how light the weight. That more orderly account is worth the price of abandoning some initial intuitions.

By comparing different situations—tables and springs, books and flies, and so on—the students confront the dilemmas of building a consistent account out of situations that intuitively seem quite different. This engages both the evidence level and the inquiry level of knowledge as discussed before. The students deal with a genuine issue in the interpretation of physical reality. Evidence enters through efforts to contrast different situations and reason about them comparatively. Inquiry enters as the students try, with the teacher's help, to construct a coherent account of a range of phenomena. Overall, the episode creates an opportunity for the teacher to bring out the students' conceptions of what physics should be like, how closely it should match their intuitions, and why or why not.

Ms. Fulton thinks that her students have grasped the notion that a higher principle, such as unity, is more valuable than holding on to one's intuitions. In doing subsequent problems, she finds, however, that they still tend to embrace their initial conceptions rather tightly, so she has to remind them of the principle discovered earlier. She explains it again and reaffirms the importance of higher level principles in science.

Meeting the Bottom Lines

Ms. Fulton's lesson meets several of the bottom lines.

Bottom Line: Use real-world examples to model higher order knowledge in a discipline. yes ■ no ☐

The use of a real world example provokes a specific instance where higher order knowledge comes into play, this time higher order knowledge of the importance of explanatory coherency in science, where a common principle knits together seemingly different cases.

Bottom Line: Provide explanation of higher order knowledge within a discipline. yes ☐ no ■

This lesson does not contain direct explanation of higher order knowledge. However, as the discussion moves toward more general principles and standards, there is ample opportunity to explicitly discuss and explain the broad, higher order canons of scientific inquiry.

Bottom Line: Encourage interaction. yes ■ no ☐

The lesson confronts students with the mismatch between their intuitions and their beliefs about what physics should be like and asks them to work through that mismatch in conversation among themselves and with the teacher. It brings their underlying conceptions about science and scientific phenomena to the fore and makes them objects for discussion.

Bottom Line: Be sure that students receive feedback for higher order knowledge. yes ■ no ☐

Upon seeing that they continue to neglect the higher order principle, the teacher provides feedback to students by reminding them of the concept and reiterating its importance.

Following Up: Integrating the Lesson into the Classroom Culture

Ms. Fulton frequently has the students revisit and refine their conception of scientific investigation. On a poster, she starts a list of principles her students discover about doing science as they gain more higher order knowledge about science throughout the year. The first word the class enters on the "Principles of Science" list is *consistency* and they work hard at coming up with a precise phrase to capture the meaning of the principle. Later, they add more terms to the list, such as *simplicity* and *universal*, along with appropriate definitions. She frequently reminds them to refer to the list and gives positive feedback when they employ these principles in their thinking.

TRASH ANTHROPOLOGY

Sally Rosinski, age eight, brings an odd "show-and-tell" to school one day—a bag of trash from a neighbor. She doesn't feel embarrassed, because several other students in the class have done the same.

Here is a list of some of the items from Sally's neighbor's trash bag:

- a cardboard tube, maybe from a paper towel roll
- a molded cardboard drink holder, maybe from MacDonald's
- an empty bag of Oatmeal Raisin Cookies
- an empty bag of Stove Top stuffing mix
- a crinkled piece of aluminum foil
- another crinkled piece of aluminum foil, stained and smelling like chicken
- a label reading jellied cranberry sauce
- a plastic wrapper labeled hearts of celery
- a MacDonald's drink cup and straw
- a plastic wrapper for a chicken
- an empty milk carton

After listing out some of the items from the trash bag, the teacher puts a challenge to the class: "What can we tell about Sally's neighbor from the trash?"

"I think there are kids," says one student. "Because of the MacDonald's stuff."

"But adults like MacDonald's too. It doesn't have to be a kid," says another.

"I think it's Thanksgiving," says a third. "It's a Thanksgiving dinner, with the chicken and all and the cranberry sauce. Thanksgiving was just last week."

"That certainly makes sense," acknowledges the teacher. "But do we have any counterevidence, any evidence on the other side."

"There's the stuff from MacDonald's," says another student. "What's MacDonald's stuff doing there if it's Thanksgiving. That's not much of a Thanksgiving dinner!"

"Maybe kids came to visit," another youngster proposes. "You know, lots of people come to visit on Thanksgiving. So maybe the kids had some MacDonald's food on the way and got rid of the trash."

The teacher keeps the discussion going for a while longer, working at the blackboard to list the proposals and the evidence for them. Finally, the teacher leads a roundup of the conclusions that the class feels are pretty certain and those that are not so certain.

Why did Sally bring in her neighbor's trash? And why did the teacher take such pains to lead the class in an analysis of it—and of a couple of other trash bags too?

"Because," the teacher explains to the class, "this is how we have to find out about an awful lot of things—indirectly, on the basis of leftovers." The teacher connects the trash bag experience with the study of ancient peoples and how we know about them. "The early cultures of the Middle East or the Native American cultures of America did not leave diaries or archives to tell us what life was like. We have to make our best guesses from the leftovers of those civilizations. In fact, anthropologists learn a lot from trash—things people of the past threw out."

The teacher takes this as an opportunity to examine with the students how anthropologists reach conclusions about civilizations long gone, by painstaking inference from indirect evidence. The teacher reviews two or three cases of inference from the leftovers of civilizations with the students, keeping alive the analogy with the trash bags. At the end, the teacher leads a discussion on how confident we should feel about such conclusions. The students agree that it all depends: Some conclusions are likely to be a lot sounder than others, just as with the trash bag.

Meeting the Bottom Lines

Ms. Rosinski's rich and in-depth lesson touches on several of the bottom lines.

Bottom Line: Use real-world examples to model higher order knowledge in a discipline. yes ■ no □

The trash activity provides a concrete close-to-home model of inference from leftovers and the basis for making an analogy with archeological investigation.

Bottom Line: Provide explanation of higher order knowledge within a discipline. yes ■ no □

The teacher deals quite directly with the problems of evidence (the evidence level) and interpretation (the inquiry level, a matter of theory building) in understanding ancient cultures.

Bottom Line: Encourage reflective engagement and interaction. yes ■ no □

The reflective engagement of the students in the trash bag activity gives them a concrete experience of analyzing indirect evidence.

Bottom Line: Ensure that students receive feedback for higher order knowledge. yes □ no ■

This lesson does not directly address issues of feedback, but it is part of following up.

Following Up: Integrating the Lesson into the Classroom Culture

The teacher continues to design lessons around accessible analogies, not only in anthropology, but around the notions of evidence and interpretation in general. For example, when a girl describes how her cat was scratched in a fight, the class examines various bits of evidence indicating that it may have tangled with a racoon. The teacher uses each example to discuss the problems of evidence and interpretation. She encourages reflective engagement and interaction whenever students are dealing with indirect evidence—figuring out when someone is angry at you, how a river became polluted, and so on. She provides a lot of feedback to students, encouraging them to consider the evidence and commending them when they do it appropriately.

PAIR PROBLEM SOLVING

How can we build students' awareness of the craft of problem solving in mathematics? Certainly the aim is a worthy one, because hardly a topic troubles students more than the solving of word problems in arithmetic and algebra. One general approach to helping students attain more awareness of the craft of mathematical problem solving was developed a number of years ago by Arthur Whimbey and Jack Lochhead. They called it "pair problem solving." (Whimbey & Lochhead, 1982).

Pair problem solving asks students to work in pairs on a problem, but assuming different roles. The students take turns in these roles for different problems. The student in the problem-solver role tackles the problem in question and "thinks aloud" in the process. The other student's job is to listen. And most emphatically *not* to interfere in the problem-solving process itself. The "listener" can ask any questions of clarification to be sure that he or she understands exactly how the problem solver is thinking about the problem.

What does pair problem solving sound like in action? Imagine that our pair of students faces this thoroughly conventional algebra problem: "Mike can mow the Millers' lawn in two hours. Bill can mow it in three hours. How long will it take the two of them working together to mow the Millers' lawn?"

The dialog between two students engaged in pair problem solving might sound something like this.

Solver: Well let's see, Mike in two hours and Bill in three. (Pauses.)

Listener: Can you tell me what you're thinking about.

Solver: I was just imagining it. Here are these two guys working together to mow the lawn. Now let's see, I suppose it's in between.

Listener: What do you mean by in between.

Solver: I mean if Mike can do it in 2 hours and Bill in 3 then when they work together it's probably some kind of average.

Listener: You mean somewhere between 2 and 3 hours, when they work together.

Solver: Yeah, somewhere between. 'Cause they're working together. Wait a minute, no, that doesn't make any sense.

Listener: Why not? What's bothering you there?

Solver: If they're both working on it, they're going to get it done faster. They should get done faster than either one of them working alone. The total time should be less than two hours. I mean, if it wasn't, Mike might as well do the whole job himself.

Listener: I see what you mean.

Solver: So I have to figure out how to put the numbers together to see how much better they can do together. It's sure not an average. Maybe if I draw a picture and imagine how it goes. (Draws sketch, with more than half labeled "Mike.")

Listener: Why are you drawing in that way?

Solver: Well, I was thinking that Mike works faster than Bill. So, if they both work on the lawn together, starting at opposite ends say, then Mike will end up doing more than Bill.

Listener: Got it.

And so on. Writing about the craft of pair problem solving in the classroom, Jack Lochhead notes that one of the principal challenges is to get the listener to stick to his or her role. At first, listeners commonly feel an almost overwhelming impulse to butt in, rather than just listening and pushing for clarity. For example, in the above example, the listener might notice what didn't make sense about the average before the solver and say, "Wait a minute, it can't be an average. Because working together, they should get the job done faster." This is just what the listener needs to learn *not* to do. The solver needs to have a chance to come to the same realization. But the listener can ask questions like, "Tell me again why the time when they're working together should be *between* the fast time and the slow time?"

Another problem is encouraging the listener truly to pay attention. One artful way of encouraging listeners to attend assiduously to the problem solvers calls for the teacher to cruise about the classroom, helping out here and there as necessary—a good thing to do anyway. When the teacher approaches a pair, the teacher asks the *listener,* not the problem solver, for an account of what's going on. It's the listener's job to have an answer ready, and listeners soon learn this. The teacher commends the listeners for performing their observation role well.

After pairs of students have worked through a problem, then the teacher might hold a general discussion about how the problem-solving process went, pointing out pitfalls and good strategies as well as going over the substance of the problem itself. The teacher listens to the students' reports of what they noticed about their own thinking and gives feedback on specific ways they can learn to watch and improve their thinking.

After several rounds of pair problem solving, playing the role of both listener and problem solver, students become more aware of the management of their own problem-solving processes. Their listening gives them a perspective on how the mind works when facing mathematical problems and opens the way for discussing the ins and outs of mathematical problem solving on the basis of direct experience.

Meeting the Bottom Lines

Pair problem solving is a powerful way to meet several of the bottom lines of teaching for higher order knowledge.

Bottom Line: Use real-world examples to model higher order knowledge in a discipline. yes ☐ no ■

The problem students tackle in the above example involves the not-so-real world of word problems in mathematics, so the discussion does not involve real world examples.

Bottom Line: Provide explanation of higher order knowledge within a discipline. yes ■ no ☐

As part of the follow-up discussion of the pair problem-solving activity, the teacher draws ideas from the students about good problem-solving tactics and adds comments as well.

Bottom Line: Encourage reflective engagement and interaction.
yes ■ no ☐

Reflective engagement and student interaction are central to this example which addresses the problem-solving level of higher order knowledge. The focus on students' own problem solving creates an opportunity for them to play out their ideas concretely, through actual examples, sharing them with the listener. Such reflective engagement helps students to sharpen their ideas about problem solving. The discussion after the pairs have worked together provides for further reflection and direct attention to the ins and outs of mathematical problem solving.

Bottom Line: Ensure that students receive feedback for higher order knowledge. yes ■ no ☐

The questions the listener poses to the solver amount to a kind of feedback, showing the solver what moves puzzle the listener and therefore might need more of a rationale. During the pair problem-solving exercise, the teacher gives positive feedback when students carry out their roles well. Later, the teacher gives them specific feedback on how to use their insights to continue learning about their own thinking.

Following Up: Integrating the Lesson into the Classroom Culture

This kind of self-examination is a powerful tool to help students gain awareness about their own thinking processes and to learn about key elements of the problem-solving level of higher order knowledge. The technique can be integrated into many areas of instruction. The key is to focus on students' reflective engagement in their own thinking as it happens and on student-to-student interaction. There is less emphasis on direct instruction, although discussions can lead to some explicit explanation of higher order knowledge. Although the primary aim of the technique is for students to gain insight into their thinking process on their own, constant feedback from the teacher is important.

WHAT FROST MEANT

Sometime in high school most students read the well-known poem by Robert Frost, "Stopping by the Woods on a Snowy Evening." It's easy to interpret this poem as expressing a kind of "death wish," a hunger to be done with the complexities of life. Frost himself denied such an interpretation point blank, claiming that it was just what it seemed to be: A poem about stopping by the woods on a snowy evening.

How does one tell what a poem means? How does one tell if an interpretation is sound? English teacher Dorothy Bear decides to seize the opportunity to get her tenth-grade students to think more deeply about evidence for an interpretation—and other sorts of evidence in other disciplines too. She's aware that some other teachers in her high school have been working to boost students' understanding of higher order knowledge in their disciplines. She decides to create an occasion for some comparing and contrasting.

Ms. Bear articulates her initial assignment this way:

> *Write an essay on the interpretation of the Frost poem. Organize it into three parts. In Part I, show how you would look for evidence of the "death wish" interpretation in the poem itself. Give some evidence pro or con. In Part II, pretend you are a historian taking a historical approach to testing the "death wish" interpretation. Say what you might do as a historian to explore Frost's true intention. In Part III, pretend you are a scientist studying how people interpret poems. Spell out an experiment you might do to test how most people interpret this poem.*

To say the least, most of Ms. Bear's students are startled by this assignment. No one has ever asked them before to think about the same topic in the style of different subject matters. Nonetheless, many of them find it intriguing. On the following Monday, they bring in their essays, and Ms. Bear conducts a class discussion around some of their ideas. She builds the discussion around a key question: "How do we proceed differently, when looking for evidence in literature, or in history, or in science?"

As the discussion develops, Ms. Bear builds a large comparison and contrast chart on the blackboard to capture a number of the points that are made. By the end, with her help, the students have identified a number of points of similarity and difference in seeking evidence in literature, history, and science.

Meeting the Bottom Lines

Focusing on comparing and contrasting the use of evidence across disciplines helps Ms. Bear touch on several of the higher order knowledge bottom lines.

Bottom Line: Use real-world examples to model higher order knowledge in a discipline. yes ☐ no ■

Ms. Bear does not model a process or introduce students to model situations where higher order knowledge is a puzzle, as with the Lexington Green or book-pushing-down-on-the-table examples.

Bottom Line: Provide explanation of higher order knowledge within a discipline. yes ■ no ☐

Through the comparison and contrast chart, the teacher draws explanations from the students as well as adding her own. The teacher thus uses the assignment to explain characteristics of the seeking of evidence in literature, history, and science.

Bottom Line: Encourage reflective engagement and interaction. yes ■ no ☐

After students write their initial essays solo, they interact in discussing the implications. Ms. Bear might have aimed to get even more interaction by having the students pair up for their initial essays.

Bottom Line: Ensure that students receive feedback for higher order knowledge. yes ■ no ☐

Feedback emerges during the discussion following up on the essay writing: students see what kinds of similarities and contrasts were raised by other students and can compare this with what they thought. Also, Ms. Bear will give students feedback on their essays.

Following Up: Integrating the Lesson into the Classroom Culture

Ms. Bear keeps this comparative enterprise alive by not only repeating this kind of activity in her own classroom, but also by engaging teachers of other subject areas within the school in similar activities. She and a social studies teacher coordinate a few assignments so that when Ms. Bear's students are studying *The Crucible*, the social studies teacher simultaneously has his students use the play as evidence to debate historical points of view. Ms. Bear tries to make similar connections with teachers of other subject areas as well. Soon students remark on how they started out wondering what these assignments were for, but now they begin to see better how the different subject matters work.

TAKING THE PLUNGE: GUIDELINES FOR INSTRUCTION

Every discipline involves some higher order knowledge, so the possibility of illuminating for students the higher order aspects of your subject matter may have already begun to appeal to you. Once you decide to begin addressing higher order concerns in the classroom, you might draw upon the following suggested plunge points.

Plunge Point #1

1. Reread the first example in this chapter, "Lexington Green," and use it as a guide for designing your own lessons.

2. Select a real-world example that represents an actual problem or type of investigation typical of the discipline you are teaching. It could be something like the discovery of conflicting results in physics, interpreting a painting, doing a proof in mathematics, generating a research question for a science fair experiment, or preparing arguments for a debate on nuclear arms. The important thing is that it embodies the authentic complexities of actual investigation in the discipline.

3. Choose an aspect of higher order knowledge you want to focus on. It could be the problem-solving level, the evidence level, the inquiry level, or a combination. Begin a dialog with your students about the thinking process involved in doing the type of investigation at hand. For example, if students are constructing a science research question, discuss with them the issue of "What makes a good question?" Together, explore the complexity of concerns—the goal of constructing theories with explanatory power, choosing questions that are worth asking, seeing how results will contribute to what is already known, determining what various outcomes would mean, and finding phenomena of interest.

4. Pick up the thread of discussion of higher order knowledge repeatedly over the course of instruction. Create lists of elements or considerations that the class discovers about the investigation process along the way. Make a point of connecting these process insights to how investigation and discourse is done in this discipline in the real world.

5. Reflect. After you have begun to engage the class in revealing some of the higher order aspects of the discipline, take stock of your progress in this new undertaking.
- Review your work with students over the past few weeks. Have you achieved a desirable balance between teaching content knowledge and higher order knowledge? Ask yourself if there are points in your teaching of content knowledge where you could address the problem solving, evidence, and inquiry levels of higher order knowledge as well.

- Ask yourself whether students appear to comprehend that there are aspects of the discipline at a higher level than the content knowledge and that these aspects represent what it means to do investigation in the discipline. Reflect on which elements they seem to understand and which they have trouble grasping.

Plunge Point #2

1. We ourselves often do not stop to consider what elements characterize the enterprise of doing investigation in the discipline we teach. Before designing lessons for your students, sit down to think about what you consider the important higher order elements. You can use the levels of problem solving, evidence, or inquiry to help construct them, if you wish. Make a list of what you consider the most important elements to highlight for your students.

2. Take your list and look over your upcoming lesson plans to find places where higher order knowledge aspects might be addressed in the course of your instruction. Make time within your teaching plans to accommodate more direct attention to higher order knowledge.

CONTINUING ON: MAKING HIGHER ORDER KNOWLEDGE A PERMANENT PART OF THE CLASSROOM CULTURE

Naturally, higher order knowledge is something that you want to become a regular and active part of students' work and activity in the discipline. Students should understand that thinking and investigation in the discipline are characterized by certain kinds of problem solving, evidence, and inquiry. To achieve this, the aim is to make higher order knowledge an ongoing part of the classroom culture. This requires devoting continued attention to the four aspects of enculturation once again.

Models of Higher Order Knowledge

- Use examples from real-world practice of the discipline to examine important higher order aspects of the discipline. Let students experience the investigative dilemmas faced by historians, artists, scientists, literary critics, and so on.
- In your everyday practice, try to model the higher order aspects of problem solving, evidence, and inquiry that you wish to cultivate in students. Use problem-solving strategies appropriate to the discipline. Provide evidence in the style of the discipline whenever you make a

claim or offer an interpretation. Explain what considerations are involved when you formulate a question or construct a theory.

Explanations of Higher Order Knowledge

- Plan lessons where you examine and discuss aspects of higher order knowledge, preferably in conjunction with concrete examples where students can engage in and reflect on the process. Talk explicitly about the kinds of problem-solving strategies employed, the kind of evidence required, and the kind of inquiry goals that are central to the discipline.
- Employ tangible devices, like lists or posters, that serve as permanent references and keep track of the important strategies, considerations, factors, standards, and concerns that make up higher order knowledge.
- When appropriate, make comparisons of the higher order knowledge inherent in different disciplines. Discuss why evidence is used differently in history, science, and literary criticism and how the goals of inquiry differ. Review ways in which they are similar.

Interactions with Higher Order Knowledge

- Design activities that maximize reflective engagement and student interaction. Employ new techniques, such as pair problem solving, to engage students in actively reflecting on their thinking processes. Capitalize on students reacting to other students.
- Build students' awareness of higher order thinking processes by allowing them to experience and reflect on the processes themselves. Refrain from intervening or offering direct explanation too early.

Feedback on Higher Order Knowledge

- Commend students when they display an understanding of higher order principles; for example, when they demonstrate that they know what constitutes good or bad evidence within the discipline. When their understanding appears weak, remind them and reinforce the higher order concepts through continued explanation and example.
- Make higher order knowledge part of the classroom culture by promoting expectations and standards for all members of the class. Students and teacher alike should give feedback on an appropriate or inappropriate display of the principle.
- Gear assignments and assessments so that students are engaged in a real inquiry situation, that is, doing an authentic problem or investigation. In that way, you can assess their grasp of higher order knowledge, not just content knowledge.

Checking Your Progress

Using a weekly chart that you complete at the week's end, you can see how well you are covering the four modes of enculturation: models, explanation, interaction, and feedback. Table 11.1 is a sample chart filled out with some possible thinking activities a teacher might have done during the week.

TROUBLE SHOOTING: QUESTIONS AND ANSWERS ABOUT HIGHER ORDER KNOWLEDGE

Higher order knowledge sounds pretty abstract. I wonder if my students are ready for it?

This is a legitimate concern. Look to the examples for some guidance; they all work to make higher order knowledge quite concrete and "experiential" for the students. Packaged in this way, higher order knowledge should make sense to most students—and make the discipline a lot more meaningful, too.

Didn't Piaget say that youngsters can't handle really abstract thinking until "formal operations" are attained, around adolescence? So perhaps higher order knowledge should wait until then.

Piaget originally proposed something like this. But an abundance of research over the past twenty years has shown clearly that Piaget, a man of many insights, overgeneralized on this one. All sorts of abstract ideas prove quite accessible to young children, *providing* (1) they are not too complex, and (2) they are well rooted in the child's experience. In other words, it is not abstractness per se that poses problems, but complexity and detachment from experience. Again, the examples presented earlier work hard to package ideas in a simple and experiential way.

Should I be spending time on higher order knowledge when my students aren't understanding all of the regular content?

This is a natural concern. It's worth recalling here a position urged earlier in the chapter: Understanding the regular content often *depends on a better grasp of the overall discipline and how it works*. In other words, we urge you not to think of attention to higher order knowledge as time stolen from content understanding. View it instead as an investment in students' content understanding.

I'm afraid that my students will be bored by attention to higher order knowledge, which seems so "philosophical."

Some will probably be bored. It's hard to keep everyone's interest all the time. But we predict that you will find *fewer* youngsters bored with the lively

continued on page 154

TABLE 11.1 Higher Order Knowledge Weekly Progress Chart

	MONDAY	TUESDAY	WEDNESDAY	THURSDAY	FRIDAY
Models			Since some students had trouble understanding their roles, I had one pair of students who were doing it well demonstrate in front of the class.		
Explanation				Starting with students' observations, I held a discussion around what is important in problem solving as well as pitfalls and strategies.	
Interaction	Had students do pair problem solving.	I had both solvers and listeners report what they felt about the thinking that went on the previous day.	Students repeated the pair problem-solving exercise using a new problem.		Each set of partners did another episode of pair problem solving; this time reversing roles.
Feedback	As I walked around the classroom, I gave students feedback on how well they were observing.	I let students give each other feedback on what they felt: observers to solvers and visa versa.			As I roamed the classroom, I gave feedback to students and encouraged students to give feedback to each other.

kinds of higher order knowledge activities discussed earlier than are usually bored with straight content lessons. For one thing, attention to higher order knowledge opens up a discipline for many students, helps it to make more sense, and awakens their interest. For another, it's simply a change of pace and many students welcome it as such.

▶12

Teaching for Transfer

> **Transfer:** *1. Acquiring knowledge in one context and putting it to work in others. 2. Applying thinking strategies and dispositions in many different contexts. 3. Connecting seemingly different areas of knowledge, seeing how they inform one another.*

In his sonnet number 19, William Shakespeare offers one of those lines that demonstrate dramatically the reach of poetry. Writing of the transience of summer, Shakespeare says "Summer's lease hath all too short a date."

Think about that line! On the one hand, we have the rich somnolence of summer. On the other hand, we have the world of lawyers, landlords, and leases. To make his point, Shakespeare brings the two worlds together, urging that we only have a lease on summer, soon to expire, and our enjoyment of summer still falls within the strict compass of "legal" requirements—the inevitable end of the season.

In these lines, as in so many others, Shakespeare demonstrates with virtuosity the human talent for transfer: connecting up knowledge from one context with another. But, of course, we do not have to be latent Shakespeares to show the art and craft of connection making. People do it all the time. For example, you learn to drive a car. There comes the time when you move from one house to another. You rent a truck and find that you can drive it well enough; your car-driving skills carry over from car driving to truck driving. Or, for example, you learn a foreign language such as French. In later years, you study Italian and make a happy discovery: You can carry over a good deal of the vocabulary *and* some useful general strategies and habits for mastering a language. Or you spend the first years of your life infighting with a sibling. You learn how to calm down and handle yourself.

Later on, you find that the same attitudes serve you well in your work setting.

Transfer, every bit of it. Transfer occurs whenever we carry over knowledge, skills, strategies, or dispositions from one context to another. Transfer occurs whenever we connect up one area of knowledge to another, to help us understand or gain leverage on a problem. Without transfer—without this connecting of one thing to another—human learning would not have anywhere near the capacity to shape and empower our lives that it does.

Therefore, transfer is fundamental to education. We do not teach youngsters to read so that they can continue to read homework assignments, but so that they can put reading to work in their lives, reading newspapers for knowledge of their world, documents for their professions, literature for pleasure and perspective, and so on. We do not teach youngsters mathematics so that they can continue to do exercises, but so that they can put mathematics to work figuring income taxes, shopping wisely, calculating engineering specifications, keeping books, and so on. We do not teach science and history to build students' quiz-taking abilities in those subjects but to equip them with ways of seeing the world and reasoning about it that empower them now and in the future. In education, transfer is the name of the game. Without full rich transfer of what students learn, education has not done its job.

Important as it is, both research and experience suggest that transfer often does not occur automatically. We need to help learners to connect up what they already know and what they learn today with where they might apply it tomorrow. But what does it look like to teach for transfer?

Anita Perez is going over a classic piece of the science curriculum with her sixth graders: the human circulatory system. She is acutely aware that this is not usually the most exciting lesson in her curriculum. Also, she feels that her students do not fully catch on to the underlying "logic" of the circulatory system: how delivery of oxygen and nutrients to individual cells throughout the body requires a massively branching set of conduits.

With these challenges in mind, Anita Perez chooses to enliven and deepen the lesson through transfer, by engaging her students in exploring analogies to refine their understanding of the circulatory system.

Ms. Perez: We've been talking about the human circulatory system by itself. Let's see whether we can think of some *other* circulatory systems that can help us to understand the human circulatory system through comparison. Where else besides in the human body do things circulate? (No response from students.) Well, for example, do things circulate in your home? Or around a city?

Student #1: There's plumbing in your home.

Student #2: There's electricity.

Student #3: Cars circulate around a city.

Ms. Perez: Yes, those all make sense. *(Ms. Perez lists the examples on the blackboard.)* Let's do a quick comparison and contrast. What do you see as a key similarity and a key difference between these cases and the human circulatory system?

Student #1: In the plumbing, well, a key way they're the same is it's liquid. And the water gets used up and waste put out—sent to the sewers.

Student #2: A key difference is it's not oxygen or food that gets delivered. It's just water.

Ms. Perez extracts two or three more key similarities and differences. Then she probes for some overarching generalizations that help to bring the logic of circulatory systems of all sorts into focus.

Ms. Perez: Let's stand back and see what we're learning from this. What's *common* to all or most circulatory systems that we're looking at?

Student #1: Usually there's some kind of pipe or thing that carries stuff. Blood vessels. Pipes. Electric wires. Streets. Something has to carry whatever's circulating.

Ms. Perez: Good. What else?

Student #2: There are *little* pipes or wires or whatever. Lots of them. Like the wiring in your house instead of the big wires in the city. Or like side streets and alleys.

Ms. Perez: Good. And why are there all those little things? And so many of them.

Student #3: Well, you see, the wires or pipes or whatever have to make contact with where you need the stuff, whatever it is, water or blood or whatever. The circulatory system has to make contact with all the cells. Or the electrical system in a city has to make contact with all your light bulbs and motors and so on. So you need lots of wires or pipes or streets.

Ms. Perez: And why lots of *little* ones? What's the logic?

Student #3: Lots of big ones would fill up all the space. There wouldn't be room for anything else.

Student #2: To deliver stuff and take stuff away from a single cell, you only need a little capillary. Or a small wire for a light bulb. Because they don't have to carry a lot. So why have them big?

WHAT IS TEACHING FOR TRANSFER?

To understand teaching for transfer, we first have to get in focus what the phenomenon of transfer involves. As the introductory examples show, transfer is a phenomenon of human thinking and learning. Transfer occurs when people acquire knowledge, strategies, dispositions, or other things that can be learned in one context—and then apply them in another context. In this way, the mechanisms of human learning and thinking make more of what is learned than they otherwise might. We get far more "mileage" out of what we learn by way of the mechanisms of transfer.

Psychologists draw a broad distinction between "near transfer" and "far transfer" (Salomon & Perkins, 1989). The contrast is not a strict one. However, roughly speaking, near transfer occurs when people apply what they have learned to a context rather similar to the context of learning. To recall an example mentioned earlier, when you learn to drive a car and then find that you can drive a truck quite adequately on moving day, this exemplifies near transfer. Driving a car and a small truck are rather similar. It is fairly easy to drive a small truck after your experiences with car driving.

Far transfer, in contrast, involves connecting up contexts that intuitively seem quite remote from one another. When Shakespeare writes of our having a lease on the summer, he relates domains that appear quite distant—summer and leases. Likewise, suppose you were an ardent chess player in your teens. Now, in business, you recall a principle from chess: Strive for control of the center. In your business investments, you interpret this to mean investing in industries that play a pivotal role in an expanding economy. Superficially at least, the worlds of chess play and business investment appear remote from one another. So this is a case of far transfer.

Psychologists also distinguish between positive and negative transfer. Positive transfer means transfer that yields positive payoffs for us, as in the cases just mentioned. But not all transfer is positive. For example, when holiday travelers rent a car in England, they find that they have to exercise great care with driving on the left hand side of the road, as England requires. Old habits tend to yield negative transfer—negative in England at least—a tendency to drive on the right. Although negative transfer does not interest us here, it is worthwhile recognizing the phenomenon.

The Somethings, Somehows, and Somewheres of Transfer

If this gives us a quick picture of transfer, what does teaching for transfer involve? Teaching for transfer simply means organizing instruction in ways that help learners to take advantage of transfer, seeing how one thing applies to another, how they might use widely what they are learning, how they can understand one thing in terms of another, and so on.

One useful way to conceptualize the opportunities for teaching for transfer in the classroom is to think in terms of the "somethings," "somehows," and "somewheres" of transfer. This framework was developed by Robin Fogarty, David Perkins, and John Barell during a series of workshops with teachers on teaching for transfer. In a single sentence, the general story of transfer can be described this way: *Somethings* are, *somehow*, transferred *somewhere*.

The *somethings* of transfer are anything students learn that might be transferred, for instance:

- Skills of reading, writing, arithmetic, working in groups, analysis—and any skills of thinking—might get transferred widely to many applications.
- Thinking dispositions, such as the disposition to be broad and adventurous in one's thinking, or clear and careful, or organized, might carry over to inform learners' behavior in many settings.
- Knowledge about history, biology, physics, or any other subject matter might provide guidance in casting a vote, making a purchase, choosing a career, watching out for a health hazard, and so on.

In building a culture of thinking in the classroom, we are of course especially concerned that the varied dimensions of good thinking—mental management, the language of thinking, the strategic spirit, and so on—transfer widely to empower learners in a diversity of settings.

The *somehows* of transfer are whatever teachers can do to cultivate transfer of learning. And there are many things, for instance:

- As in the example of the circulatory system, engaging students in identifying and exploring analogies and making generalizations that get at the "common logic" of the topic at hand (for instance, circulatory systems of all sorts).
- Anticipating applications: Brainstorm with students who are acquiring a skill (say, essay writing or a decision-making strategy) about where else they might use it, and why, and how they would have to adapt it.
- Providing diverse practice: Have students actually practice very different applications of a piece of knowledge, a strategy, a skill, or a disposition. Use role playing and similar tricks to introduce variety.
- Transfer *in:* In teaching a topic, recognize that students often already know something about the topic or related topics from everyday life. Engage the students in connecting up the new topic with what they already know about it. For example, although the biological taxonomy

of plants and animals may be new to students, they know many classification systems from everyday life—addresses, for instance, which describe a place by way of the state, the town, the street, and the house number—that can help them to understand the logic of hierarchical classification.

The *somewheres* of transfer are the choices teachers have about the targets of transfer, where to transfer *to*. Roughly speaking, the opportunities fall into three categories:

- The same subject matter: Instruction almost always invites efforts to transfer ideas within the same subject matter. What, for instance, does the French Revolution tell us about the American Revolution? This is "near" transfer.
- Different subject matters: As the current and welcome enthusiasm for integration across the curriculum demonstrates, there are myriad opportunities to connect the subject matters up, discovering how they inform one another. For instance, the mathematics of population growth have a lot to say about the history of exploration as well as historical problems of famine.
- Life outside of school: In the long term, we do well to remember that youngsters' experience within school aims to serve their lives outside of school. Even in the short term, ideas students acquire in school can help them outside it. Arithmetic can prove useful in supermarket purchases. History can help in understanding the morning newspaper. Biology can help in monitoring one's diet. And so on.

WHY IS TEACHING FOR TRANSFER IMPORTANT?

Most educational practice betrays a mistaken assumption: Transfer takes care of itself. Throughout their educations, students acquire a variety of knowledge and skills. Teachers, administrators, and parents all tend to presume that students will carry over what they learn to other settings.

Unfortunately, both everyday experience and a variety of laboratory studies show just the opposite. The transfer we want often does not occur spontaneously. Learners are plagued by the problem of "inert" knowledge and skill—learning stored up in memory that does not get activated in useful circumstances. We know the knowledge or skill is there; students disclose it if directly tested for it. But it might as well not be there for all the good it does students when they face out-of-school problems or open-ended tasks in school, such as writing an essay or planning an experiment.

Some psychologists have drawn a very pessimistic conclusion from such results. They have proposed that the human mind harbors little potential for transfer. Learning needs to be packaged discipline by discipline, topic by topic. There's little payoff in trying to help students to connect things up.

However, a more careful examination of the mechanisms of transfer and the findings on transfer presents a much more encouraging picture. In some laboratory studies, substantial transfer has occurred. In some efforts to develop students' critical thinking abilities, they have shown clear signs of carrying over these abilities and attitudes to other settings. Transfer is not at all a lost cause.

What does emerge clearly is that transfer cannot be counted on to occur spontaneously. If we educators want transfer, we need to teach for transfer. We need to engage youngsters in applying their knowledge and skills in deliberately varied contexts, so that they learn how widely what they have learned can be put to work. And we need to help students to think about the ideas they are learning and make deliberate connections across subjects and between school and out-of-school contexts. Teaching for transfer becomes a serious responsibility for every educator.

THE BOTTOM LINES: INCORPORATING TRANSFER INTO THE CULTURE OF THE CLASSROOM

So now to the bottom line—what does teaching for transfer require? How can you, the teacher, tell whether or not you are giving due attention to teaching for transfer as part of building a culture of thinking in the classroom? Here are some simple tests to apply. If you can move toward saying "yes" to these bottom lines regarding teaching for transfer, you know that you are serving students well so far as transfer is concerned.

1. Provide models of transfer. When planning the teaching of a topic, spend time thinking about what "somethings"—knowledge, skills, strategies, dispositions—invite transfer, and think about what "somewheres" to encourage transfer to. Illustrate for students how people, including yourself, transfer knowledge, skills, and dispositions from one situation to another. Note examples of how transfer occurs within a subject, across subject matter, and in everyday life.

2. Explain the need for transfer, as well as particular connections, helping students to anticipate applications. Emphasize how vital the ability to carry over knowledge, skills, and dispositions is to learning and daily life. When teaching a topic, commit some discussion time to *anticipating applica-*

tions: thinking about where students they might use what they are learning and what it would be like to use it there. Also, ask students directly to seek connections between the topic and other things it connects to, within the same subject matter, in different subject matters, or in everyday life.

3. **Interact with students and provide opportunities for them to interact with one another around transfer.** Engage students in discussions and activities where transfer can be encouraged through interaction with you and one other. When students engage in any kind of practice, take care that the practice is *diverse:* Use very different examples representing very different kinds of applications, so that students are encouraged to map what they are learning widely.

4. **Give feedback that promotes transfer and revisit transferred ideas.** Offer recognition when students show evidence of transferring knowledge, skills, strategies, or dispositions from one situation to another in class. After teaching a topic, take pains to revisit transferrable ideas soon (the next day, the next week) and again later (in a few weeks), to reinforce transfer from the topic. Encourage students to recognize and remark when other students make good connections.

Chapter 13 provides classroom examples, instructional guidelines, and tactics for enculturating transfer.

13

Teaching for Transfer: Pictures of Practice

Chapter 12 outlined the importance and key elements of teaching for transfer. This companion chapter offers practical examples of how to teach in a manner that promotes transfer. On the following pages appear several sample lessons, as well as guidelines for instruction, tactics for enculturation, and troubleshooting advice. In preview, the upcoming sections are:

1. **Atoms**
   This example shows a teacher helping students to understand the concept of atoms more deeply through comparison with other cases where we break things down into a small number of constituent parts—such as the letters of the alphabet.

2. **Truman and Decision Making**
   President Harry Truman's famous decision to drop the atomic bomb on Japan presents an occasion to develop a perspective on history as a sequence of decisions and to cultivate students' decision-making skills, with plenty of transfer both to further history studies and students' personal lives.

3. **Inquiry Diaries**
   This activity confronts the daunting fact that students' understanding of science often clings more closely to the textbook and exercise sheets than to their perception of the everyday world. The inquiry diary helps students to see the world through "physics-colored glasses."

4. **What Story Speaks to You?**
   A simple essay activity helps students find personal connections with the literature they are reading.

5. **Being Careful**
   Trivial errors are a persistent problem in youngsters' arithmetic performance—even though many youngsters have considerable knowledge in principle about what to do to eliminate errors. Here, a teacher builds a program of error elimination over several days, relying on strategies for more careful computation that the students themselves can identify.

6. **Taking the Plunge: Guidelines for Instruction**
   A suggested starting point for beginning to promote transfer in your classroom teaching.

7. **Continuing On: Making Teaching for Transfer a Permanent Part of the Classroom Culture**
   Recommendations for making teaching for transfer a permanent part of the classroom culture.

8. **Troubleshooting: Questions and Answers about Teaching for Transfer**
   Common obstacles to teaching for transfer and what to do about them.

ATOMS

Suppose you are teaching a lesson on "atoms." You are Jill Busby, about to face your fourth-grade students and introduce them to one of the most fundamental scientific ideas in the curriculum.

You know that the notion of atoms is not an easy one. It is natural for the youngsters to learn to go through the motions of a few glib answers about everything being made of atoms. But do they really understand the idea of atoms?

You sit down to think about the notion of atoms yourself. Anticipating teaching for transfer, you ask yourself, *What is powerful and general about atoms?*

It's not hard to see. The key idea seems to be that everything is made of a few things. All matter is made of atoms of just a few kinds, the chemical elements. *A powerful idea,* you think to yourself. *Everything made of a few things.*

You decide that you have an opportunity here to help your students toward a deeper conception of what atoms are all about. There are many contexts where we break down everything into a few things. The letters of the alphabet are the "atoms" of spelling, for instance. The digits are the "atoms" of numbers. You resolve to work with your students to get them to recognize this general, powerful idea.

Your students have read about atoms in their textbook. When it's discussion time in class, you launch a discussion along these lines.

Ms. Busby: You know, we can often understand things better by connecting them with other things. It really works. It's a good tool for understanding. Let me show you what I mean.

Let's concentrate for a few minutes on the key idea of atoms. Here's what I think that key idea is. There are many things in the world: water, apples, fingers, flowers, stones. But they are all made of the same few things, like building blocks. They are all made of a few kinds of things called atoms, the different kinds of atoms. It's really amazing.

You know, this idea of finding that lots of things are made of just a few things is very basic. I can think of another example—the alphabet. Can you tell me what I mean by that, how the alphabet is like atoms?

Student #1: Yeah, I guess. It's like the letters are the atoms for words. I mean, we only have twenty-six letters. But we can made any word at all out of them.

Ms. Busby: Very good. So we've found a way to break down any word we can say into a few letters and write it with just a few letters. Now, let me give you a challenge. Can you find anything else that's like that? Anything else where you have complicated things made of just a few basic things?

Student #2: Numbers are another example. They're sort of like letters.

Ms. Busby: Good. What else.

Student #3: Legos are like that. When you build things out of Legos, you can build all sorts of things. But really there are only a few kinds of Legos.

Student #2: How about houses. I mean, you have doors, and windows, and pipe, and boards, and a few things like that. And that's all there is.

Ms. Busby: Good again. So you see there are many things like that. Now why do you think this is a powerful idea? *(No response from students.)*

Let me explain my question a little more. Why is it a good idea to see things as made up of a few simple kinds of things. Why bother?

Student #1: Well, it makes things simpler in a way. You know what you're working with.

Student #3: You know that whatever you have, it just has to boil down to these few things.

Ms. Busby continues to explore the theme with her students a little while and then moves on with the rest of her lesson.

But she wants to keep the idea of breaking things into a few standard parts alive. The next day, the students look at the parts of atoms more carefully—electrons, protons, neutrons, and other subatomic particles. Ms. Busby takes this as an occasion to revisit the idea of standard building blocks, one level down. When her students talk about molecules in a few days, she will revisit the concept yet again, in that setting. And she will try to get her students to recognize multiple levels of chunking in other things that they know about. For instance, if letters are the atoms of words, then words are like molecules that make up larger units—sentences and paragraphs.

In "somethings transfer somehow to somewhere" terms, Ms. Busby has chosen the "something" as the general idea of decomposition into building blocks, the "somehow" as discussion in which the students explored analogies, and the "somewhere" as many familiar examples from everyday life, such as the alphabet.

Meeting the Bottom Lines

Ms. Busby's engaging and thoughtful lesson on atoms meets all of the bottom lines of teaching for transfer.

Bottom Line: Provide models of transfer. yes ■ no □

Ms. Busby provides the example of the letters of the alphabet as an initial model of the building blocks concept. Her students take it from there.

Bottom Line: Explain the need for transfer as well as particular connections, helping students to anticipate applications. yes ■ no □

Ms. Busby emphasizes the usefulness of connecting things up as a tool of understanding.

Bottom Line: Interact with students and provide opportunities for them to interact with one another with transfer.
yes ■ no □

Ms. Busby engages her students interactively, drawing out other examples besides the alphabet connection.

Bottom Line: Give feedback that promotes transfer and revisit transferred ideas. yes ■ no □

During the discussion, Ms. Busby gives positive feedback to students as they begin to think of connections between atoms and things they are familiar with. She revisits the idea of decomposition into building blocks later in the context of subatomic particles and then in the context of molecules, extending students' understanding of it.

Following Up: Integrating the Lesson into the Classroom Culture

Ms. Busby continues to plan her lessons with the "something, somehow, and somewhere" of transfer in mind. For several weeks, she sticks with the same building block notion but expands the approach. In several subsequent sessions she asks students to generate more connections and analogies having to do with building blocks. Later, she has a discussion with them about why it might be useful to make connections among things that are similar in structure. To diversify the activity, she has students do an art project where they think of something made up of smaller parts and create a montage representing the structure. She herself begins to realize what wide relevance the building block concept has and continues to revisit the idea throughout the year, making more and more distant connections.

TRUMAN AND DECISION MAKING

In the spring of 1945, President Harry Truman faced one of the most fateful decisions of modern history. He pondered whether or not to order the dropping of the atomic bomb on Japan. Few would like to face such a decision, but it was Truman's job. As he said on another occasion, "The buck stops here."

Truman was not pleased with the dilemma of the use of the bomb. To his biographer William Hillman, he had this to say (Hillman, 1952):

> *I gave careful thought to what my advisors had counseled. I wanted to weigh all the possibilities and implications. Here was the most powerful weapon of destruction ever devised and perhaps it was more than that. . . .*
> *I then agreed to the use of the atomic bomb if Japan did not yield.*
> *I had reached a decision after long and careful thought. It was not an easy decision to make. I did not like the weapon. But I had no qualms if in the long run millions of lives could be saved.*
> *The rest is history.*

The Core Lesson

As with many other pivotal moments of history, this was a moment of decision. Many teachers concerned to bring decision-making skills and strategies into play in their classroom have chosen this among other historical episodes as arenas within which to work. The core lesson one can build around the Truman decision is almost transparent: Truman made a decision.

We, resisting our temptation to judge as Monday morning quarterbacks, can try to remake the same decision, using information from texts and other sources that profile the circumstances of the times.

If the students for such a lesson have not yet received any instruction in decision-making strategies, such instruction becomes part of the presentation. In chapter 9 we discussed a "ready-made" decision-making strategy that easily applies here. Adjusted for this context, the basic steps in decision making include:

- *Generate options imaginatively.* Thus, students are encouraged to generate many actions that Truman might have taken, getting beyond the simple either/or of ordering the bomb dropped or proceeding with a land invasion.
- *Assess options carefully in terms of consequences and costs/benefits.* Thus, students are asked to predict the possible consequences of various plans, ask whether those consequences appear likely or not so likely and why, and appraise the costs and gains.
- *Reach a decision, balancing all factors.* Thus, students are asked to make Truman's decision again, judging which factors weigh most in the balance.

A lesson such as this, in keeping with building a culture of thinking in school settings, strives to bring together a deeper understanding of history as a process of decisions made by individuals with a deeper appreciation of and skill at the process of decision making itself.

But here is the key question: What about transfer? Nothing in the "core lesson" attends directly to the transfer either of the historical understanding or of decision-making strategies. With this in mind, here are some additional elements that attend to the matter of transfer in various ways.

Before the Core: Connecting to Personal Experience

Developed by Robert Swartz, a colleague of ours and a well-known scholar in the critical thinking movement with extensive experience working with teachers, a question sequence something like this serves well to awaken students to the challenges of decision making.

R. Swartz: Did any of you make any decisions today?

Students: Sure. *(They name several.)*

R. Swartz: Sure. We make decisions all the time. Let's talk about your decision making a little bit. Any of you make any decisions during the last week or month that didn't work out so well? *(Several students raise their hands.)*

Let's see if we can explore a couple of questions about these decisions. What went wrong? And how could you have thought about it differently in order to make a better decision in the first place?

Student: Well, I wrote my name in a driveway we just had paved. But it was really expensive to get it out. My parents were really mad.

R. Swartz: Okay. So it was pretty expensive. Well, how could you have thought differently to make a better decision in the first place?

Student: I could have thought more about what might happen. About how hard it might be to get out.

R. Swartz: Yeah, that makes sense. So we can write down, "Think about how hard to get writing out."

Robert Swartz takes three or four more cases from students, jotting on the blackboard how the students might have thought differently in order to make a better decision. The answers tend to fall into two categories: considering more options and looking more carefully at consequences. He underscores these at the end.

An activity like this, done before an activity like rethinking the Truman decision, connects the Truman decision with everyday dilemmas of decision making and demonstrates to students the unity of the decision-making enterprise in contexts great and small.

After the Core: Connecting to More History

After students rethink the Truman decision, what then? Is that the end of the lesson? If you are teaching for transfer, it should not be. The idea of decision making provides a powerful lens for examining the course of history.

One natural follow-up is to treat another episode of history in the same fashion. President John F. Kennedy's handling of the Cuban Missile Crisis would be a natural candidate, for example. This can be done in class, or through an essay assignment, perhaps with students working together in groups to manage the complex ins and outs. For yet more flexibility, you can ask students to form groups and each select an episode from history.

After the Core: Connecting to Another Subject

Decisions invite study in other subjects besides history. In English, many stories hang on a character's decision at an important turning point. In science, policies about protecting ecologies or controlling recombinant DNA research have a basis in our understanding of the natural world. In the visual arts, studio records of works like Pablo Picasso's *Guernica* reveal the artist making key decisions to develop a work one way rather than another. If you teach more than one subject, or can collaborate with a teacher of another subject, you have ample opportunity to engage students in analyzing one or more decisions across subject matters. Students may have a more difficult time anticipating distant applications and making connections across subject areas, so you might model transfer by working through an example that illuminates the similarities across situations.

After the Core: Connecting to Personal Decision Making

How about relating decision making to one's own life? An easy way is to ask students to keep a "decision diary" for a week. They log the decisions that they consider the more important ones and even write out some of their decision-making process in their diaries. They can keep out of the diary any decisions they feel self-conscious about.

At the end of the week, the students form pairs or trios, exchange diaries, and talk about their decision-making experiences.

In terms of "somethings transfer somehow to somewhere," these ideas around Truman's decision highlight two "somethings": the notion of history as a series of often painful and complex decisions, and the craft of good decision making. The "somehows" include discussion, analysis, and rethinking of decision-making episodes. The "somewheres" encompass students' everyday lives and episodes from history. It would be easy to expand the "somewheres" to decision points in literature (Hamlet's *indecision* and ultimate decision, for instance) and in other subject matters.

Meeting the Bottom Lines

This example, with its starting point on Truman's difficult decision, meets all of the bottom lines of teaching for transfer.

Bottom Line: Provide models of transfer. yes ■ no ☐

Relating students' personal decision making ("Before the Core") to the Truman lesson (the core lesson) provides students with an initial model of connecting making.

Bottom Line: Explain the need for transfer, as well as particular connections, helping students to anticipate applications.
yes ■ no ☐

As described, this cluster of lessons involves no explicit advocacy of transfer, but particular connections are explained. It would be easy to add a direct discussion of transfer and its importance.

Bottom Line: Interact with students and provide opportunities for them to interact with one another with transfer. yes ■ no ☐

The cluster of lessons emphasizes teacher/student and student/student interaction about transferring a decision-making framework to many settings.

Bottom Line: Give feedback that promotes transfer and revisit transferred ideas. yes ■ no ☐

Students receive self-feedback as well as feedback from each other in the decision diary activity. Ideas about decision making are revisited repeatedly through the numerous different approaches on the topic.

Following Up: Integrating the Lesson into the Classroom Culture

This set of lessons presents a diverse yet cohesive structure for teaching for transfer that can be implemented in an ongoing way in the classroom. The key element involves committing class time to connecting the subject matter topic with a diverse range of "somewheres"—other situations within the subject matter, across subject matters, and in students' personal lives. The "somehows" of the teaching approach should include direct explanation about transfer, group discussion, teacher modeling, student interaction and group activities, engagement in diverse practice, and ample feedback. Over the course of the curriculum, one might try to achieve transfer of different "somethings," from skills and strategies to content or higher order knowledge to dispositions.

INQUIRY DIARIES

Consider these excerpts from a diary:

Nov 19 I noticed how hard it is to open the post office doors. They are big doors, maybe eight feet tall and made of metal. You really have to lean into them to push them open. This is because of inertia. The doors have a high mass, so it is hard to accelerate them. When I push on them, this tries to accelerate them.

Nov 23 My dad and I watched the Patriots play this afternoon. While I was watching, I thought a little bit about physics and football. The football makes a parabola, like we learned for the trajectories of missiles. You can see its parabola shape on the television, when the cameras point in the right way. The linemen are chosen to be heavy because they have more inertia. It's high mass again. They just knock smaller players out of the way.

Nov 26 I saw an accident today, not the accident itself, but afterward. A car had run into a telephone pole. No one seemed to be hurt. But the front end of the car was all scrunched up. It sounds kind of cold-blooded, but I was thinking about this from a physics standpoint. The car has lots of kinetic energy. When the car hits the telephone pole, all this kinetic energy gets converted into compressing the front end of the car. It's like compressing a giant spring that stores kinetic energy. Only the compressed front end of the car doesn't spring back. So the kinetic energy doesn't get stored in the front end of the car. I'm not sure where it goes.

Ron Costello wrote these observations to go with his high school study of physics. Shortly, he will turn in his "inquiry diary," as will the other students in his class. His teacher will go over the diaries to appraise how well the students have succeeded in connecting up physics concepts with everyday observations.

Ron rather enjoys keeping the inquiry diary. It helps the physics to make sense. Before beginning the diary, Ron felt that the physics he was studying mostly sat there in the book and had very little to do with everyday events. Now he is beginning to see that physics pervades ordinary life. Major concepts of physics shape to a startling extent what happens in the world. Physics makes a difference.

Ron's teacher introduced the inquiry diaries recognizing that this would be a problem for the students. Very often, instruction in the sciences (as well as other subject matters) tends to remain encapsulated in the textbook and classroom, a kind of learning ritual where students learn certain performances and serve them up to the teacher on demand. The inquiry diaries are the teacher's way of pressing students to make some of the everyday connections that rarely turn up in ordinary education.

In terms of "somethings transfer somehow to somewhere," the "somethings" for the inquiry diary are the concepts of elementary physics, especially the qualitative concepts rather than the formulas and the arithmetic. The "somewhere" is, of course, everyday life. The inquiry diary itself provides the "somehow," the vehicle for connecting up the formally and academically presented concepts in the physics textbook to experienced physical reality.

Meeting the Bottom Lines

The inquiry diaries as described here touch on two of the four bottom lines of transfer.

Bottom Line: Provide models of transfer. yes ☐ no ■

The part of this activity described, keeping the diary, involves no provision of models by the teacher. In introducing the inquiry diary in the first place, the teacher certainly would offer examples.

Bottom Line: Explain the need for transfer, as well as particular connections, helping students to anticipate applications. yes ■ no ☐

The inquiry diary provides a structure for helping students to find applications of physics principles in their everyday lives, because the task of keeping the diary asks students point-blank to anticipate applications.

Bottom Line: Interact with students and provide opportunities for them to interact with one another with transfer. yes ☐ no ■

This is not part of keeping the diary itself, a solo activity. However, the teacher could easily arrange for the students to discuss their diaries with one another, as well as have some general class discussions.

Bottom Line: Give feedback that promotes transfer and revisit transferred ideas. yes ■ no ☐

The teacher reviews the students' diaries and provides feedback on how well they have succeeded in connecting physics concepts with everyday observations. Almost automatically, physics concepts studied several weeks ago get revisited, as students search back in the textbook to find more ways to generate diary entries.

Following Up: Integrating the Lesson into the Classroom Culture

There are many follow-up activities one could do to build on the inquiry diary. For example, the teacher might also keep an inquiry diary himself that he shares with students as a model. As noted above, entries from inquiry diaries can become subjects for class discussion, involving, for instance, how pervasive physics concepts are and how knowledge of them can be transferred from one situation to another. The teacher might direct students to anticipate applications by thinking of other potential instances of the concepts. Student interaction and feedback could be structured around small groups who exchange diaries and discuss their findings. The teacher would continue to review and give feedback on the diaries as well.

WHAT STORY SPEAKS TO YOU?

Assignment: *Review the stories that we have read over the last several weeks. Choose one that you think is especially meaningful. Write a well-organized two-page essay—introduction, body, conclusion—discussing your reasons for choosing the story, explaining what you have learned, and exploring how you think those ideas will be relevant in your future. Give evidence that the story says what you think it does.*

One Friday, the students in an eleventh-grade English class receive the above assignment. The teacher tells his class that often literature becomes much more meaningful when we make connections between the world the author creates for us and our own lives or those of our friends and families. "This assignment asks you to do just that," the teacher says. "Let me give you an example." He proceeds to tell them about a short story he recently read. He discusses why it was significant to him and spells out a couple of ideas from it that he wants to take to heart. Then he asks the students to bring their essays in on Monday.

One student chooses George Orwell's "Shooting an Elephant," reflecting the period of Orwell's life when he was an English police officer in India. This student writes that Orwell himself was a "victim of tyranny," even though in a sense one of the tyrants. Another student, responding to Heinrich Boll's "The Laugher," writes about laughter as a mask. Another student, selecting D. H. Lawrence's "The Rocking Horse Winner," notes how actions backfire—"If you try too hard to make other people happy, you end up hurting yourself."

A teacher in the Boston, Massachusetts, area uses assignments like this to engage his students more deeply in literature. Most assignments in literary studies turn to the work itself—its structure, characters, development, and so on. In this assignment, however, the teacher deliberately invites students to make connections with their own personal lives and what counts as significant to them. Notice, though, that the teacher is not ready to let the students treat the work just as a point of departure and spin their own fantasies. The assignment asks students to cite evidence from the work substantiating their viewpoint.

Students respond to this invitation positively and thoughtfully—and sometimes with startling emotion. When they hand their papers in, the teacher comments on their interpretations of the stories and the personal connections they make, sometimes suggesting other connections as well.

In "somethings transfer somehow to somewhere" terms, the "somethings" are ideas about the human condition expressed in the stories that students have read. The "somehow" is the occasion the essay provides for deliberate connection making. The "somewheres" are the students' lives.

Meeting the Bottom Lines

The writing assignment provides this teacher with a powerful way of touching on several of the bottom lines.

Bottom Line: Provide models of transfer. yes ■ no ☐

The teacher models making a connection between a short story he has read and his own life.

Bottom Line: Explain the need for transfer, as well as particular connections, helping students to anticipate applications. yes ■ no ☐

The teacher explains that making connections with one's life is a good way to get more out of literature.

Bottom Line: Interact with students and provide opportunities for them to interact with one another with transfer. yes ☐ no ■

This activity does not feature interaction, although it could easily be built into follow-up activities.

Bottom Line: Give feedback that promotes transfer and revisit transferred ideas. yes ■ no ☐

The teacher provides feedback on the connections the students make. In addition, it would be easy to organize pairwise discussions where students react to one another's papers.

Following Up: Integrating the Lesson into the Classroom Culture

The study of literature is rich in opportunities for students to make connections between stories and everyday life. Additional assignments could encourage students to connect key elements of stories to their personal experience or even situations in other subject areas. For example, students might be asked to relate conflicts expressed in a literary work to similar conflicts experienced by historical figures. Classwork should continue to encourage students to anticipate applications of things they discover or know. Transfer of ideas can be explicitly examined, discussed, and revisited with students.

BEING CAREFUL

Fourth-grade arithmetic is a minefield of trivial errors, Marjorie Rossi decided after seeing the mistake-filled exercises turned in by her students.

A little planning and plotting led her to the conclusion that she could build a greater self-consciousness about the hazards of errors and the tactics of more careful work in her students. She started off this way:

Ms. Rossi: You know, simple mistakes are a general problem that we all face when we're doing arithmetic problems. It's easy to make a slip, even when you basically understand what you're doing. How many here would like to make a lot fewer mistakes than they do? *(Most of the students put up their hands.)*

Sure you would. Okay. So let's see if we can do some strategic thinking about how not to make simple mistakes. I'm going to start a list on the blackboard of things you can do. Let's be practical now. What do you actually do to avoid mistakes?

Student #1: You work slowly.

Ms. Rossi: Fine, that's one possible thing. *(She writes it down.)* What else?

Student #2: You check your work!

Ms. Rossi: Good. And *how* do you check your work? What do you do?

Student #2: Well, you can do each problem twice.

Student #3: Maybe we could check our work with one another somehow.

Student #1: There are tricks for certain kinds of problems. We can learn those tricks.

Marjorie Rossi continues her conversation with her students until an impressive list of tactics for more accurate work adorns the blackboard. But how to get her students to take some of these ideas to heart?

Ms. Rossi: Now I'd like each of you to take a blank sheet of paper. We have lots of ideas on the blackboard. Number your paper with 1, 2, 3, and 4. Pick four of these strategies that you particularly like. And let's resolve in the next week that you're really going to try to put these to work.

Transfer within Mathematics

Ms. Rossi is pleased to discover that her students can identify strategies to help them work with more precision. But she knows all too well that most of the students who today enthusiastically diagnosed their slips will forget about it tomorrow. She needs to work with the students to keep their strategies alive and in use.

The next day, Ms. Rossi uses part of her arithmetic class to give some point-blank practice with the strategies. Before they begin, the students review the sheets on which they have written their favorite strategies. Then Ms. Rossi hands out a sheet of exercises. "Use the tricks you chose," she says. "And each time you use one, put a little check beside it."

For each of the next couple of weeks, Marjorie keeps the idea of careful work on the minds of her students. One day she asks them to write their four tricks at the top of the exercise sheet and put check marks every time they use one. Another day she asks the students to compare notes with one another: How are their strategies working? Would they like to take up someone else's that they think might work better? Another day she reads the answers aloud, has students self-correct their papers, and then asks them to pick mistakes they made and figure out why their strategies didn't help them to avoid those mistakes.

Soon, she finds that her students are a lot more self-conscious about precision in their arithmetic work. And they are making many fewer errors!

Transfer to Other Subject Matters

Meanwhile, her students' progress has made her more ambitious in their behalf. *Quite likely,* she says to herself, *they have problems of precision in other subject matters as well.* Maybe she could do something to encourage transfer there. One day, she broaches the matter with her students: "The strategies we've been practicing for working more carefully in math—I've been thinking that they might help in other subject matters too. What do you think of that?"

Somewhat to her surprise, a few students have already made the connection. "Math is math," one says, "even when it's in science. So I use the same tricks there." Another has reached even further: "You know, things like checking work just as well when I do my grammar exercises for English. I catch my own mistakes better."

With this encouraging response, Ms. Rossi decides to steal a few minutes from her math class for the sake of the rest of the curriculum. She asks her students to make a point of using their strategies for working carefully in at least one other subject matter. And each student has to write a brief note explaining how well it worked.

"But," says one student, "some of our strategies don't really fit English. For instance, when you add to check subtraction or multiply to check division."

"True," Ms. Rossi acknowledges. "So don't pick English. Pick science. Or do pick English and use those strategies that make sense for English."

"But that's like extra homework," another student protests.

"Not so much extra," says Ms. Rossi. "Because you can do it while you're doing your work for other subjects. And it will help you there. But I guess that writing the note is extra. So I'll knock three problems off the Friday problem set, in place of your note." It's worth it, she thinks to herself, to get her students applying their strategies more broadly.

In "somethings transfer somehow to somewhere" terms, concerned about her students' arithmetic performance, Marjorie Rossi focused on the "somethings" of strategies for precise, careful work in arithmetic. Her first "somehow" to foster transfer was to keep the strategies on students' minds in different contexts for several days through a variety of activities. Then she added another "somehow," asking her students to try their strategies in another subject matter and report back. Her "somewhere" was arithmetic of all sorts in her class, and eventually other activities in other classes that call for careful work.

Meeting the Bottom Lines

With the exception of modeling, Ms. Rossi's approach touches on all of the transfer bottom lines.

Bottom Line: Provide models of transfer. yes ☐ no ■

Modeling is not part of Ms. Rossi's approach as presented above. It would be easy to add such an element, of course.

Bottom Line: Explain the need for transfer, as well as particular connections, helping students to anticipate applications. yes ■ no ☐

Ms. Rossi explicitly advocates being careful in diverse contexts. She looks to her students, too, for explanations by asking them to explain helpful strategies for various circumstances.

Bottom Line: Interact with students and provide opportunities for them to interact with one another with transfer. yes ■ no ☐

Besides interacting with Ms. Rossi, the students have opportunities to interact and compare notes with each other about the strategies they are working on.

Bottom Line: Give feedback that promotes transfer and revisit transferred ideas. yes ■ no ☐

Ms. Rossi builds in a great deal of student self-feedback by having students check off strategies they use, reflecting on how well they worked, and writing notes about how successful their transfer of strategies is.

Following Up: Integrating the Lesson into the Classroom Culture

Ms. Rossi integrates transfer in the culture of her classroom by continuing to do many of the things started in this lesson. She discusses with students how strategies can be applied in many situations, has students continue to write visual reminders for themselves, allows time for students to reflect on how well strategies work in different situations, lets students compare notes and give each other feedback, engages students in diverse practice across subject areas, and frequently revisits transferred strategies over time in different situations.

TAKING THE PLUNGE: GUIDELINES FOR INSTRUCTION

By its nature, transfer is central to learning in any field or endeavor. You may already recognize its importance but have little experience in directly teaching for transfer. Here is one general path for entering into the direct teaching of transfer. Of course, you may think of other ways that better suit you, either based on the examples included here or your own experience.

Plunge Point

1. Choose a "something" that you wish students would transfer into new situations. It could be a strategy for decision making or some other kind of thinking, a piece of content or higher order knowledge, a disposition, or something else.

2. Think about the relevance of the "something" to a wide variety of situations—within your subject area, across other subjects, and in everyday life. After you sum up the potential "somewheres," plan a range of situations to which you'd like to foster transfer.

3. Reread the example "Truman and Decision Making." Using the example as a guide, decide how you want to introduce the core lesson. Make sure students understand the core lesson before moving onto transfer situations.

4. Introduce another situation in which the "something" is relevant, for example, connect it to students' personal experience. Explain the importance of transferring things learned in one situation to another. Let students anticipate applications and make connections between the core lesson and the new situation.

5. In subsequent lessons, add multiple occasions for transfer within the subject area, across subject areas, and in everyday life so that students have diverse practice in transferring the "something."

6. Always allow adequate time for explicit discussion of the connections that become apparent to students and provide opportunities for interaction and feedback. Consider having students keep diaries as a way of recording and reflecting on the connections they discover. You can use the diaries as vehicles for self-feedback, for teacher feedback, or as objects for student exchange.

CONTINUING ON: MAKING TEACHING FOR TRANSFER A PERMANENT PART OF THE CLASSROOM CULTURE

To infuse teaching for transfer into the culture of your classroom, you need to harness the four cultural forces. Here are some general moves that can help.

Models of Transfer

- Model transfer yourself. When you carry over something you know or a useful strategy or a habit to a distant situation, or make an interesting connection between different sides of your life, alert students to the occasion of transfer and describe why the carryover is valuable.
- Direct students' attention to examples of transfer. Since transfer is something that occurs in everyday life, they can serve as their own models of transfer. Ask them to think of examples where they make connections, transferring knowledge from one situation to another in their daily lives. Relate that to the kind of transfer you are teaching them to do in class. Use other models of transfer as well, including famous people, civilizations, or even animal behavior.
- Plan for wide relevance. In advance, think about the "somewheres"— the situations within the subject matter, across subject matter, and in personal life—to which you wish to see students achieve transfer.

Explanations of Transfer

- Explain to students the importance of transfer to effective learning. Let students imagine what would happen if there were no transfer and how that would limit learning and functioning in countless ways.

- Create visual reminders for students to think about transfer. Generate lists of things to transfer, for example, lists of strategies, higher order knowledge principles, or dispositions. Encourage students to create written reminders for themselves, as students did in the "Being Careful" example.

Classroom Interactions with Transfer

- As well as providing explanations, draw explanations from your students of possible applications of what they are learning. Let them think about and discuss where they might use what they are learning and what it would be like to use it there.
- Structure activities where students interact with issues of transfer. Let students discuss and assess how well their transfer is going. Have them exchange written work such as inquiry diaries so they can talk about their experiences and give feedback.

Feedback about Transfer

- Provide positive feedback when students successfully make a transfer from one situation to another. Especially commend them when they anticipate applications and when they make distant but appropriate connections. Use small group work where students can give feedback to one another.
- Revisit transferred ideas repeatedly under a variety of circumstances. Make a point of revisiting transferred ideas soon (the next day, the next week) and again later (in a few weeks) to reinforce transfer from the topic.

Checking Your Progress

Using a weekly chart that you complete at the week's end, you can see how well you are covering the four modes of enculturation: models, explanation, interaction, and feedback. Table 13.1 on page 182 is a sample chart filled out with some possible transfer activities a teacher might have done during the week. In this sample case, the teacher has already been working for a while with students on building the strategic spirit and the disposition to be broad and adventurous in their thinking. They have practiced searching broadly for alternative options, evaluating choices, and elaborating on possibilities in the context of decision making. Now the teacher wants to foster transfer of the same strategies and disposition to other situations. This is how her progress goes for the week.

TABLE 13.1 Teaching for Transfer Weekly Progress Chart

	MONDAY	TUESDAY	WEDNESDAY	THURSDAY	FRIDAY
Models		We interpreted poems. I briefly modeled searching for alternative interpretations.			
Explanation	I reviewed the strategies and broad thinking disposition covered earlier. I asked students to think of times in daily life where these strategies might be useful.	I suggested they use what they know about searching for options. They practiced generating alternative interpretations.	In an essay assignment interpreting another poem, I told them to write down the SEARCH, EVALUATE, and ELABORATE steps on their papers as a reminder.	In my students' science class, they designed plant experiments. I suggested to the science teacher that he have them use the search strategies to decide what variables to test.	
Interaction	Students suggested situations and together evaluated whether searching for options strategies would help.	They were surprised at first to see the applicability of the strategies to poetry interpretation. We discussed this.			
Feedback				On yesterday's essays, I gave students written feedback when they displayed transfer of strategies.	The students said they were amazed when our search ideas were applied in science class.

TROUBLESHOOTING: QUESTIONS AND ANSWERS ABOUT TEACHING FOR TRANSFER

Isn't it hard for an activity to touch all of the "bottom lines"?

Yes, it is. And there's no need for a single activity to do so. In fact, if you'll look back over the five activities offered by way of a sample, you'll find that they generally do not receive a positive score on every single bottom line. If you try for several of the bottom lines frequently, you'll be doing fine in teaching for transfer.

Often activities like this call for drawing ideas from my students. What if my students don't *have* ideas to offer.

In making up activities like this—or using these—you have to make judgments about the sorts of questions that your students are likely to be able to answer. If an activity seems too demanding in that regard, redesign it or use another one.

However, beware of underestimating how responsive your students can be. In our experience, students prove much more able to answer open-ended questions than you might think—especially if given a good chance. Here are two tricks to get the best out of your students:

- Give your students a sample answer or two if they don't readily come up with answers. For instance, if students are not quite sure how to respond when you ask them about strategies for being careful in arithmetic, you might say, "Well, one thing you can do is go slowly. Another thing is have a friend check your work. There's two. What *else* can you think of?"
- Give your students time to think rather than expecting instant answers. You might even say, "Take a minute to talk with a neighbor while I make a place on the blackboard for your ideas." By the time you have the blackboard ready, there are usually several hands up.

I only teach one subject, so how can I deal with wide-reaching transfer?

Transfer doesn't necessarily mean transfer to other disciplines. Transfer is very important within disciplines. When you teach a key concept in mathematics, you want students to apply it to later chapters, to next year's curriculum, to solving problems flexibly. When you teach about the French Revolution, you want it to illuminate later studies your students make of the American Revolution or even the industrial revolution. Students often do not make these connections spontaneously.

Also, as a teacher of history, mathematics, or some other subject, you're not just concerned with students' performance in school. You want them to take their skills and understandings beyond the walls of the school and put them to work in making sense of the world around them and acting effectively within it. Students are not likely to do this unless you teach in ways that encourage it. In sum, even if you only teach a single subject matter, teaching for transfer is important.

I'm concerned that teaching for transfer will take time away from my teaching of the subject matters themselves.

Suppose that transfer activities *do* eat somewhat into your time for covering your subject matter. Ask yourself where your priorities lie. If you've thought through what transfer you'd like to see, you've asked yourself what aspects of the topic that you are teaching have wide relevance and invite transfer—the promising "somethings." Now, if you're worried about whether you have time to attend to them, remember that they are the items you identified as having wide relevance. Do you want to trade them for a narrower treatment of the subject matter?

Yes, sometimes teaching for transfer can mean a little (not usually a lot) less time spent focusing on the subject matter in the most conventional sense. But it's worth the trade! Why are we teaching unless we are highlighting powerful knowledge, concepts, skills, strategies, and dispositions, and helping students to connect them up to the "somewheres" where they will do the most good?

▶ 14

Pulling It All
Together: From
the Thinking
Classroom to the
Thinking School

PERCHANCE TO DREAM . . .

Every educator dreams about how learning and teaching might be better. As the authors of this volume, our own dreams center around thinking classrooms and smart schools. We like to imagine a school in which every classroom is a vibrant culture of thinking, a place where critical and creative thinking are valued and encouraged from all quarters. And we like to imagine how the qualities of these thinking classrooms might be woven into the texture of the school itself, so that the entire school reflects a culture of thinking, from the conversations in the cafeteria to the bulletin boards on classroom walls.

In fact, such dreams are not pure fantasy. While there are certainly serious problems in American education, there is a lot of good, too. Over the years we have met many superb educators and seen countless examples of enlightened, thinking-centered teaching and learning. These experiences have informed and inspired our dreams, and from them we have created a montage—half reality, half fantasy—of what a day in a school system that integrates several dimensions of a culture of thinking might look like.

INTEGRATING THE SIX DIMENSIONS OF THINKING: A VISION

Often one sees elementary and secondary school buildings in close proximity to one another—next door, or on the same plot of land. Such an arrangement is appealing, because it facilitates cross-grade interaction and supports a feeling of community. Let us imagine a thinking-centered school clustered in this way: On a single city block there is a central building with several out buildings. All together, the buildings house grades one through twelve. The following pages describe an envisioned visit to such a school. In this visit, we observe how the six dimensions of thinking described in this volume come together to create an overall culture of thinking.

A Day at Central School

On the morning we visited Central School, the first thing we noticed was a blackboard outside the main office with the heading "Things I Wonder about Today" printed across the top. Below the blackboard was a sign that read:

All those with questions: Record what you wonder about here. Identify yourself if you would like people to respond.

The following items were written on the blackboard:

I *wonder why the middle line in the road is painted yellow.* (Sheila Grafton, grade 4)
I *wonder if myths and legends get changed when people remember them and tell them to their grandchildren.* (Carlos Vilas, grade 8)
I *wonder why the president can't do something about all the guns and gangs.* (Tanika Firth, grade 11)
I *wonder if there is a way to make algebra more interesting for my students.* (Mr. Cozeman, teacher, grade 10)
I *wonder why people get electricity in their hair.* (Ashley Patnaude, grade 5)

The superintendent, Ms. Simon, was in the process of adding a line of her own to the blackboard. "Hi!" she said, seeing us. "Welcome to Central School. You're probably wondering what this blackboard is all about. Just let me get my thought down, and I'll explain it to you."
Ms. Simon finished writing the sentence:

I wonder whether anyone has any ideas about how to keep us from tracking so much mud into the school buildings. (Ms. Simon, superintendent)

"There," she said, brushing the chalk off her hands. "You know, one of the things we try to encourage in our school is thinking dispositions—dispositions like open-mindedness, the strategic spirit, and inquisitiveness. We want to do more than build students' thinking skills; we want to help students develop the *urge* to think critically and creatively. I guess you could say we want our students and staff to have 'attitude'—a *thinking* attitude."

"Sometimes schooling can stifle students' natural curiosity," Ms. Simon continued. "But at Central School we believe that the inquiring spirit is at the heart of learning. So we encourage anybody in the school to write a question here on this blackboard. And we encourage anybody who has an idea about any question to go and talk to its author. You'd be surprised how many conversations get their start here. For instance, I expect to hear some good ideas about mud control before the day is through. And I guarantee you that Ashley, our fifth grader, will learn at least something today about static electricity."

Reflection: We were impressed by Ms. Simon's blackboard. It did indeed seem like a powerful way to cultivate the disposition to inquire, and it did so by making use of two of the tenets of enculturation: It was a model *of a thinking disposition, because it was an in-action example of people wondering and inquiring; and it* facilitated *interaction, by providing an open invitation for the entire school community to share their curiosities and engage in inquiry with one another.*

Ms. Simon said that the school was expecting us: we were free to wander about the buildings and enter any classroom. We asked where we could find the elementary grades. "First building on the left," she said. "Have fun!"

Mr. Vargas invited us into his fourth-grade class with a smile. He explained that the class was in the middle of a unit on weather and climate.

"The children have just finished a project in which they recorded daily weather conditions over the course of a week and compared their observations with television weather reports," he said. "I like to encourage my students to be good mental managers. So before we started the project, we thought together about our goals and standards. Now, when we are done with the project, our list of goals help us reflect on our work. In fact, we are just finishing our reflections. We were just talking about what went well with our projects, and what was hard."

Mr. Vargas turned back to the class and pointed to a list of goals on a bulletin board. "Does anyone have any more reflections about how their project went?" The bulletin board said:

THINKING GOALS

- Be organized
- Be curious: notice interesting things
- Be neat when you make your weather chart
- Be patient
- Don't be afraid to ask questions

A dark-haired girl raised her hand. "One thing that went well for me was that I noticed something interesting. I noticed that when you are using a thermometer to measure the temperature, it makes a big difference how close to the house you are. See, at first I put my thermometer on the outside of my bedroom windowsill. Then I wondered what would happen if I measured the temperature at the back fence, too. So I did, and all week there was about 5 degrees difference in the two temperatures—it was always warmer near the house.

"An interesting observation," Mr. Vargas said. "Let's take a minute to think about it. What reasons might there be for the difference in temperatures?"

The fourth graders discussed the issue, and several theories were proposed: Maybe the color of the house absorbed the sun and made the air around it warmer, said one student. Maybe the back fence was in the shade and made the air there cooler, suggested another. As Mr. Vargas moderated the discussion, we noticed that he used lots of language of thinking words— words like *reasons* and *investigation* and *observation*—and encouraged his students to do the same. Eventually the discussion drew to a close, and Mr. Vargas posed his students this question:

"What connections can you make between the project you just did and other things in the world that you know about?" he asked. "How can what we just studied help you to think about other things? Take time to think before you answer, because this is a hard question."

After a moment, Mr. Vargas asked for ideas. At first, the children didn't have much to say, but the discussion grew lively when one student pointed out that recording the temperature is like having the job of being a weatherman, and that you could learn about other things by doing other kinds of jobs.

"Like you could write a report of a real accident, as if you were a newspaper reporter," he said. "Then you could learn about what it would be like to be a reporter."

"Yeah, or you could look for bones and stuff as if you were an archaeologist," said another student. "That would help you learn about archaeology."

When we left Mr. Vargas's classroom, this discussion was still ongoing.

Reflection: Four dimensions of good thinking seemed to be present in Mr. Vargas's classroom. First, as Mr. Vargas himself explained, he was trying to encourage mental management, and indeed his students were practicing good mental management by reflecting on their thinking goals. Second, the goal list aimed to encourage thinking dispositions. Goals like 'be curious' and 'be organized' are very spirited, and seemed likely to encourage dispositional patterns of thinking. Third, throughout the interactive class discussions, Mr. Vargas used a rich language of thinking, and, by modeling it for his students and giving them feedback, he encouraged them to use it, too. Finally, Mr. Vargas incorporated teaching for transfer into his lesson, by explicitly asking his students to make connections between the project they just did and other things they knew about.

We visited a few more elementary classrooms and continued to see evidence of a vibrant culture of thinking. For example, in one second-grade class, students were about to begin studying their neighborhood. "Before we start," said the teacher, "let's brainstorm two different kinds of ideas about our neighborhood: One, think about all the things you are certain about; and two, think about all the things you need to investigate." The teacher explained the meaning of the words *certain,* and *investigate.* Then, he modeled the words in use: "For example," he said to his students, "I am *certain* that we have many different kinds of people in the neighborhood—African Americans, European Americans, Hispanics, and more. But I don't know where these groups came from or why, so I need to *investigate.*

In addition to the obvious emphasis on the language of thinking, this second-grade class brought to mind our earlier discussion with the superintendent about the thinking disposition of inquisitiveness. Often, learners see themselves as the passive recipients of information. But by asking students what they need to investigate, this second-grade teacher sends his students an important message about how the inquisitive spirit can play an active role in learning.

Late in the morning we left the elementary school and crossed the courtyard to the building that housed the middle school grades. We entered the building and immediately heard the sounds of an animated discussion. We took the liberty of knocking on the classroom door from whence the voices came, and a teacher greeted us.

"Welcome and come in," he said. "This is an eighth-grade health class. We were just discussing food labeling. In particular, we were wondering about the food labels that say things like 'healthy selection,' and 'all natural,' and 'good for you.' Are they? I mean, are they really good for you, as the labels claim?"

The teacher turned back to his students. "Where were we?" he asked.

The class resumed a vigorous discussion. Clearly, this was a hot issue.

"Of course they're good for you," a student insisted. "The labels can't say that unless they are."

"Yeah, sure," countered a more cynical voice. "Labels can say anything they want."

"No they can't," someone else objected. "There are laws!"

"Yeah, but the laws aren't always right. Sometimes the government thinks something is okay for you, and then later you find out it causes cancer or some other disease."

The discussion continued for another minute or so, then the teacher broke in.

"Hold on here. It looks like we've got a pretty messy issue on our hands. How can we get organized about thinking this through? What will help us focus?"

The class was silent for a moment. Then a student said:

"Hey, how about making up a thinking strategy? You know, out of those strategy building block things."

The teacher agreed that was a good idea. He asked students what the steps in the thinking strategy should be.

"Well, first we need a 'state' step," one student suggested, "where we state exactly what the issue is and what we want to do about it."

The teacher wrote "state the issue" on the blackboard. After some discussion, students stated that the issue was whether to believe labels that claimed certain foods were good for you.

A student at the back of the room suggested that the second strategy step should be "reasons, for and against."

"We should try to say all the reasons we can think of to believe the food labels," she explained, "and all the reasons we can think of *not* to believe them."

The class agreed that this was a good next step. The teacher suggested that at this step they should also give evidence for their reasons.

"I know what evidence in science is," said one student. "But what do you mean by evidence here?"

"Evidence is an example, or some sort of information or proof, that supports your reason and makes it more believable," he explained. "For instance, earlier Lydia said that people shouldn't believe the labels because the food companies might be lying. Lydia, do you have any evidence for that claim? In other words, do you know something that gives us reason to think that the food companies might lie?"

Lydia, a slender girl in the back of the room, furrowed her brow. "Well, yes. But not really strong evidence. Haven't you ever heard of false advertising? Everyone knows that some companies don't tell the truth in their advertising. So food companies might be like that, too."

"Thanks, Lydia. You used a good phrase there, when you said that you had evidence, but not strong evidence. You're right to suggest that evidence can be strong, or weak, or in between."

The class embarked on a lengthy discussion of reasons. As students spoke, the teacher continued to urge them to provide evidence for their views. We left the class just as the discussion of reasons was coming to a close. As we were leaving, we heard one student insist that the next strategy step should be "investigate."

"Listen," he said, "we've got a whole bunch of reasons up on the board. We should *do* something with them. We should investigate the situation. Let's figure out a way to actually go and find out whether the food labels tell the truth."

We thought that sounded like a pretty good idea.

Reflection: Three dimensions of good thinking appeared in the health class: (1) the strategic spirit, (2) higher order knowledge, and (3) the language of thinking. As to the strategic spirit, the teacher had obviously taught students about the strategy building blocks previously and had provided practice in their use. Attention to higher order knowledge—knowledge about solving problems and seeking evidence—showed in the way students were learning to deal with the problem of knowledge acquisition in the area of health education. And the language of thinking occurred, particularly when the teacher spoke of reasons and evidence.

*Cultural forces were at work, too. The teacher provided **explanations** when necessary, for example when he explained the concept of evidence. He also provided informative **feedback** about the language of thinking, when he praised Lydia's use of the phrase "strong evidence" and explained what is good about it. And of course there was plenty of **interaction** in the classroom—students were building a thinking strategy together, pursuing higher order knowledge interactively, and all the while using key terms and concepts from a language of thinking.*

At lunchtime, we stopped for a bite to eat in the middle-school cafeteria. At a nearby table was a group of students, two of whom we had noticed in the health class this morning. We couldn't help overhearing a bit of their conversation.

"I don't know what to do about it," one student said. "I used to swim in that river all the time. But the color of the water has changed: it looks polluted. I think one of the factories upstream is dumping stuff in it."

"Are you sure?" a worried voice asked. "I mean, how do you know? What's your evidence?

"Well, the water's a weird color. That's evidence. I guess it's not strong evidence. Still, it makes me nervous. I'd like to find out what's going on."

Another student chimed in. "Hey, let's do something about it. Let's *investigate.*"

At this point, the din of the cafeteria obscured the students' conversation. But we couldn't help smiling. It was nice to hear students using the language of thinking among themselves, without the prompting of a teacher. And it was good, too, to hear the stirring of the strategic spirit. Central School was beginning to seem quite impressive.

After lunch, we strolled over to the high-school building. Just inside the main door, we found the computer lab. About twenty students were working in pairs in front of computers. We introduced ourselves to the woman who seemed to be in charge. "Hi, I'm Jill Haddad," she said. "You probably think I'm the computer teacher, but actually I signed up the computer lab for my algebra class today. Take a look. Feel free to ask questions."

Standing behind a pair of students, we saw that they were entering algebraic equations to make different graphs. One student entered the equation $Y = X^2$ and a parabola appeared on the screen. "Now let's see what happens if we add 5 to it!" The student entered $Y = X^2 + 5$. A parabola of the same shape appeared, but 5 units higher on the screen. "It moved up five," the other student said. "That makes sense. Now lets try adding an X term, like $Y = X^2 + X + 5$ maybe."

"What are you guys working on?" we asked the students.

"Well, see the idea is Mrs. Haddad wants us to know how different changes in an equation like this one make different changes in the graph. Like when we added 5 the graph moved up 5 units."

"Do you know what changes to expect?"

"No. She said experiment and find out what the rules are."

"So why is that important to learn?"

"Well, Mrs. Haddad says over and over that equations and graphs are two different ways of showing the same function. But equations make some things easier to see about a function and graphs make other things easier to see. Like it's easy to see whether a graph goes through the origin, but you have to look at the equation and figure it out, whether it does or not. So anyhow the idea is Mrs. Haddad wants us to go back and forth easily between graphs and equations."

"So you're experimenting."

"Yeah, we're experimenting. We're supposed to find out what kinds of changes in the equation make what kinds of changes in the graph."

"Well, great, keep it up." We turned back to Mrs. Haddad. "That's really interesting. It's almost as though you've turned your math class into a science class; you're having them experiment and generalize."

"Yes, that's right. You know, there are rules in the text for what happens when you change various parameters in an equation. But I really want them to get a feel for it by messing with it themselves. But actually I want to make a point about proof and evidence too."

"How will that happen?" we asked.

"Well, the students are going to come up with rules based on their experience with the computers. But then I'm going to ask, 'How can we be sure those rules are really absolutely valid.' I know what they're going to say. They're going to say, well, 'we tried it five or six times.' But then I'm going to say that in math that isn't good enough. When we see a regularity, we want to *prove* that it has to be that way logically, for instance by algebraic manipulation."

"So you're going to have your students try to do that."

"Yes, that's step two of the activity. And I know from past years that most of them will be able to write out proofs in algebra of the generalizations they make. But what I find most fun about this is the discussion we then have about what proof is for and why trying it five or six times isn't good enough."

"Do you think they'll be convinced?"

"Some of them. But really, it's a running theme, one of several that we keep coming back to, how mathematics works as a system."

"Do the students know about step two yet?" we asked.

"Not really," said Mrs. Haddad. "I just told them to find some rules and then we'd do something with them."

We turned back to the two students. "How are you doing?"

"Fine. We have a rule about what moves the graph up and down—that's the constant term. And now we're working on the X term and what that does. It moves the graph around slantwise, and we're trying to figure out what's going on."

"Then what?"

"Oh, Mrs. Haddad is going to ask us to prove stuff. She always does that. She really wants us to nail things 'cause partly that's what math is about, proof and all."

We told Mrs. Haddad her students were wise to her game. "That's good," she said. "They're catching on to how math works, at least around me." We thanked Mrs. Haddad and left the computer lab.

Reflection: Clearly higher order knowledge of mathematics was alive and well in Mrs. Haddad's class. She had engaged her students in mathematical inquiry. As a further step, she planned to help them toward an understanding of the role of formal proof in mathematics. The students had begun to catch on to this theme: They could predict that questions of proof would come next. The language of thinking also put in a appearance in the students' use of terms like experiment, rules, and prove.

In the next hour, we looked in on several other classrooms in Central High. We walked into the middle of a spirited debate about whether poetry taught one anything relevant to life. We heard a bit of a straightforward but extremely clear lecture—rich with the language of thinking—from a social studies teacher about how immigrant populations have influenced American culture and what predictions we could make for the future. We observed a chemistry lab, where one trio of students was engaged in an all-out brainstorm to try to figure out why an experiment that should have worked didn't. In a European history class, we encountered a formal debate between two halves of the class about the chances for a European common market succeeding, in light of a history of rivalry and ethnic differences.

In the gym, we discovered the coach encouraging students to make up their own calisthenics. The coach would say, "Let's work on legs. So what can we do that's different. Stretch your thinking—be inventive."

At last we found ourselves back at the "Things I Wonder about Today" blackboard outside the main office. There were more entries on the blackboard now. For one thing, Ashley Patnaude's question had grown a tail. Now this is what it looked like:

I wonder why people get electricity in their hair. (Ashley Patnaude, grade 5)

It's friction. Rubbing balloons on cloth does the same thing. (Jackie, grade 6)

I know that, but why does friction do it? (Ashley)

It's just in cold weather mostly. (Mary D., grade 4)

It has to do with electrons and how they get rubbed off things. (signed Electron Man)

Come by room 112 in the high school building right after school and I'll give you a couple of explanations to try on for size. You can even test them. All welcome, including Electron Man. (Jerry Tanner, physics teacher)

With this, the school day ended and so did our visit. As we were leaving Central School, we stopped to say good-bye to Ms. Simon. We asked her how the school came to be so interested in the teaching of thinking. She explained that the faculty has been working on it for quite a while—five years or so. It all started with one fourth-grade teacher, named Ray Vargas. He was the first to get excited about teaching students to be better creative and critical thinkers, and originally his aim was simply to create a strong culture of thinking in his own classroom. But the idea spread, as good ideas are prone to do, and soon several other teachers in the school became interested. Mr. Vargas shared his materials with the rest of the school, and helped interested colleagues to incorporate dimensions of good thinking into their own classroom cultures.

"Ray had no idea he would start something with such momentum," Ms. Simon said. "More and more teachers came to him for advice. Even now, he is frequently invited to other school systems to talk about what we are doing here. In fact, a few years ago, in response to this interest, Ray distilled some of his advice into a short set of seven start-up guidelines—a checklist of sorts—for teachers to use as they began experimenting with the six dimensions of good thinking."

We asked Ms. Simon if it would be possible to see Mr. Vargas's checklist. "Sure," she said, and gave us a copy to take with us (see Appendix).

As we left Central School, we looked back at the buildings and marveled at the fact that within such plain exteriors thrived a truly vibrant culture of thinking. With no more resources than most other cities and towns, Central School had transformed itself into a community in which students were encouraged to be thoughtful learners and trained to be powerful thinkers. Of course, such an achievement does not come easily: the faculty of Central School had undertaken an enterprise that involved high aspirations and plenty of hard work. Yet, as we thought about the era in which Central School's students would come of age, we felt a wave of gratitude for the faculty's aspirations. Because nothing less would do.

Mr. Vargas's Start-up Checklist for Creating a Culture of Thinking in the Classroom

1. Identify the things you already do in the classroom that touch on any or all of the six dimensions of thinking and build on them, making use of the four cultural forces.

Most teachers already address some aspects of the six dimensions while teaching. For example, you may already be teaching for transfer by encouraging students to look for intercurricular connections. If so, ask yourself what you can do to more vividly model the spirit of transfer. Ask what you can do to more explicitly explain the purpose of transfer and its associated tactics. How can you give students more informative feedback about the transfers of knowledge they currently make? What more can you do to involve students in interactive activities around connecting knowledge to new contexts?

2. Learn as you go. Start experimenting with one thinking dimension at a time and be alert to how it naturally draws in others.

Focusing on one dimension will naturally pull in aspects of others. For example, suppose you want to encourage the strategic spirit in students. So you decide to teach them a thinking strategy, perhaps a decision-making strategy. In the process, you find yourself using key language of thinking terms like reasons and evaluate. Then, as students are using their newly learned strategy, you notice that they get a little sloppy in their thinking. So you remind them to be good mental managers and show them a couple of tactics for monitoring their thinking as they work. This kind of interconnectedness comes about naturally and reflects the integrated nature of good thinking. Noticing how different dimensions of good thinking interweave can also help you find good points of entry for giving a new dimension special attention.

3. Start small. Think big.

Great initiatives often fail because of unrealistic expectations early on. The classroom is a busy place. Select a thinking dimension to focus on that fits well with your other instructional goals and plan how you will incorporate it into a series of lessons. At the same time, recognize that the idea of a culture of thinking is a big, pervasive idea: if you continue to give it attention, ultimately your teaching and your classroom will be transformed in a powerful way. Start with manageable goals, but be ready to expand your efforts as new possibilities are revealed.

4. Be explicit with students about what you are trying to do: Make cultural change a joint effort.

For each thinking dimension that you introduce into the classroom, straightforwardly explain to students what you are trying to do and why you are trying to do it. For example, if you are focusing on mental management, explain to students what mental management is, why it is an important part of good thinking, and what you will be trying to teach them. Whenever possible, elicit students' help in seeking opportunities to focus on any of the six dimensions. For instance, once you have explained the purpose of mental management, encourage students to actively look for, and alert you to, mental management opportunities in the classroom.

5. Whenever possible, work with colleagues.

It is very difficult to work solo, without the input and support of others. Find colleagues in the school community who share your enthusiasm about creating a culture of thinking. Work together. If possible, design lessons and units collaboratively. If close collaborative design work is not possible, share with others what you yourself have done and solicit each others' advice and feedback. Working with others will not only help you in your own classroom efforts, it will help to set in motion a schoolwide culture of thinking.

6. Try to use the thinking dimensions as bridges across different subject matters.

For those of you who teach more than one subject, aim to explore thinking dimensions in different subjects simultaneously. For example, if you are focusing on the language of thinking in social studies, make a point of also exploring the language of thinking in science. For those of you who only teach one subject, encourage a colleague to give attention to a thinking dimension you are working with, so that the dimension functions as a point of integration in the curriculum. For example, if you teach math and decide to give attention to mental management, invite a teacher in another area (such as language arts) to emphasize mental management, too.

7. Be bold: Don't be afraid to plunge in and experiment with thinking-centered activities, even if you feel unsure about exactly what to do.

Don't feel that you have to be an expert before you start! If these ideas seem abstract to you, it is probably because you haven't yet had any practical experience with them. The only way to get practical experience is to plunge in and try something in your class. Be adventurous! Choose a thinking dimension that appeals to you and design a lesson around it. Nothing can go seriously wrong and the chances are very good that you will discover that the six dimensions, once you start giving attention to them, have a momentum of their own. Acknowledge that some degree of preliminary uncertainty is unavoidable and look forward to learning as you go.

References

Bennett, P. (1970). *What happened at Lexington Green?* Menlo Park, CA: Addison-Wesley.

Bereiter, C. & Scardamalia, M. (1985). Cognitive coping strategies and the problem of inert knowledge. In S. S. Chipman, J. W. Segal, and R. Glazer, (eds.) *Thinking and learning skills, vol. 2: Current research and open questions,* pp. 65–80. Hillsdale, NJ: Erlbaum.

Binet, A. & Simon, T. (1905). Methodes nouvelle pour le diagnostic di niveau intellectuel des anormaux.: *Année Psychologique, 11,* 191–244.

Clement, J. (1982). Students' preconceptions in introductory mechanics. *American Journal of Physics, 50,* 66–71.

Hillman, W. (1952). *Mr. President.* New York: Farrar, Straus & Giroux.

Langer, E. (1989). *Mindfulness.* Menlo Park, CA: Addison-Wesley.

Olson, D. R. & Astington, J. W. (1990). Talking about text: How literacy contributes to thought. *Journal of Pragmatics, 14*(5), 705–721.

Palincsar, A. S. & Brown, A. L. (1984). Reciprocal teaching of comprehension-fostering and monitoring activities. *Cognition and instruction, 1,* 117–175.

Perkins, D. N. (in press). *Mindware: The New Science of Learnable Intelligence.* New York: The Free Press.

Perkins, D. N., Goodrich, H., Tishman, S., & Owen, J. M. (1994). *Thinking connections: Learning to think and thinking to learn.* California: Addison-Wesley.

Perkins, D. N. & Simmons, R. (1988). Patterns of misunderstanding: An integrative model of misconceptions in science, mathematics, and programming. *Review of Educational Research, 58*(3), 303–326.

Pressley, M., Borkowski, J., & Schneider, W. (1987). Cognitive strategies: Good strategy users coordinate metacognition and knowledge. In R. Vasta & G. Whitehurst (eds.), *Annals of child development* (vol. 5), pp. 89–129. New York: JAI.

Pressley, M., Johnson, C., Symons, S., McGoldrick, J., & Kurita, J. (1989). Strategies that improve children's memory and comprehension of text. *Elementary School Journal, 90*(1), 3–32.

Salomon, G. & Perkins, D. N. (1989). Rocky roads to transfer: Rethinking mechanisms of a neglected phenomenon. *Educational Psychologist, 24*(2), 113–142.

Schoenfeld, A. H. (1985). *Mathematical problem solving.* New York: Academic Press.

Sternberg, R. J. (1985). *Beyond I.Q.: A triarchic theory of human intelligence.* New York: Cambridge University Press.

Tishman, S., Goodrich, H., & Mirman Owen, J. (1990). FourThought. *Teaching Thinking and Problem Solving, 12*(4), 1–11.

Whimbey, A. & Lochhead, J. (1982). *Problem solving and comprehension.* Hillsdale, NJ: Lawrence Erlbaum Associates.

Williams, B. (1977). *Albert's Toothache.* New York: E. P. Dutton.

Further Reading

The following list is provided for readers interested in exploring further the main topics discussed in this book. Since several of these topics represent somewhat new perspectives on the teaching of thinking, entries in some sections are more sparse than others. By the same token, virtually all of the topics discussed in this book have their roots in prior work in cognitive psychology and the teaching of thinking, and the imaginative reader will make many connections beyond the works listed here. The following readings are not offered as an attempt to comprehensively list all relevant sources, but rather as an effort to indicate points of entry through which interested readers can pass, in order to forge their own paths of inquiry.

CHAPTERS 2 AND 3: A LANGUAGE OF THINKING

Theory

Astington, J. W. & Olson, D. R. (1990). Metacognitive and metalinguistic language: Learning to talk about thought. *Applied Psychology, 39*, 77–87.
Olson, D. R. & Astington, J. W. (1993). Thinking about thinking: Learning how to take statements and hold beliefs. *Educational Psychologist, 28*(1), 7–24.

Practice

Costa, A. L. (1991). *The school as a home for the mind.* Palatine, IL: Skylight Publishing.
Costa, A. L. & Marzano, R. (1991) Teaching the language of thinking. In A. Costa (Ed.), *Developing minds: A resource book for teaching thinking, Volume 1.* Alexandria, Virginia: ASCD.

CHAPTERS 4 AND 5:
THINKING DISPOSITIONS

Theory

Baron, J. (1985). *Rationality and intelligence.* NY: Cambridge University Press.
Ennis, R. H. (1987). A taxonomy of critical thinking dispositions and abilities. In J. B. Baron & R. S. Sternberg (Eds.). *Teaching thinking skills: Theory and practice,* pp. 9–26. New York: W. H. Freeman.
Langer, E. (1989). *Mindfulness.* Reading, MA: Addison-Wesley.
Paul, R. W. (1990). *Critical thinking: What every person needs to survive in a rapidly changing world.* Rohnert Park, CA: Center for Critical Thinking and Moral Critique, Sonoma State University.
Perkins, D. N. (in press). Mindware: The New Science of Learnable Intelligence. New York: The Free Press.
Perkins, D., Jay, E., & Tishman, S. (1993). Beyond abilities: A dispositional theory of thinking. *The Merrill-Palmer Quarterly, 39*(1), 1–21.
Scheffler, I. (1977). In praise of the cognitive emotions. *Teachers College Record, 79,* 171–186.

Practice

Barell, J. (1991). *Teaching for thoughtfulness: Classroom strategies to enhance intellectual development.* NY: Longman.
Facione, P. A. & Facione N. C. (1992). *The California Critical Thinking Dispositions Inventory.* Millbrae, CA: California Academic Press.
Tishman, S., Jay, E., & Perkins, D. N. (1993). Thinking dispositions: From transmission to enculturation. *Theory Into Practice. 3,* 147–153

CHAPTERS 6 AND 7:
MENTAL MANAGEMENT

Theory

Brown, A., Bransford, J., Ferrara, R. & Campione, J. (1983). Learning, remembering, and understanding. In P. Mussen (Ed.), *Handbook of Child Psychology, Vol. 3.* New York: Wiley & Sons.
Forrest-Pressley, D. L., MacKinnon, G. E. & Waller, T. G. (1985). *Metacognition, cognition, and human performance, Volume 1: Theoretical Perspectives.* Orlando, FL: Academic Press.
Palincsar A. S. & Brown, A. L. (1984). Reciprocal teaching of comprehension-fostering and comprehension-monitoring activities. *Cognition and Instruction, 1*(2), 117–175.
Scardamalia, M. & Bereiter, C. (1985). Fostering the development of self-regulation in children's knowledge-processing skills. In S. F. Chipman, J. W. Segal, & R.

Glaser (Eds.) *Thinking and learning skills, Vol. 2: Research and open questions* (pp. 563–577). Hillsdale, NJ: Erlbaum.

Schoenfeld, A. H. (1987). What's all the fuss about metacognition? In A. Schoenfeld (Ed.), *Cognitive science and mathematics education.* Hillsdale, NJ: Erlbaum.

Weinert, F. & Kluwe, R. (Eds.) (1987). *Metacognition, motivation, and understanding.* Hillsdale, NJ: Erlbaum.

Practice

Costa, A. L. (1991). *The school as a home for the mind.* Palatine, IL: Skylight Publishing.

Forrest-Pressley, D. L., MacKinnon, G. E. & Waller, T. G. (1985). *Metacognition, cognition, and human performance, Volume 2: Instructional practices.* Orlando, FL: Academic Press.

Perkins, D. N., Goodrich, H., Tishman, S., & Owen, J. M. (1994) *Thinking connections: Learning to think and thinking to learn.* California: Addison-Wesley.

Swartz, R. J. & Perkins, D. N. (1989). *Teaching thinking: Issues and approaches.* Pacific Grove, CA: Midwest Publications.

Tishman, S., Goodrich, H., & Mirman Owen, J. (1990). Fourthought. *Teaching Thinking and Problem Solving, 12*(4), 1–11.

CHAPTERS 8 AND 9: THE STRATEGIC SPIRIT

Theory

Nickerson, R., Perkins, D. N., & Smith, E. (1985). *The teaching of thinking.* Hillsdale, NJ: Erlbaum.

Pressley, M., Forrest-Pressley, D. L., Elliott-Faust, D. & Miller, G. (1985). Children's use of cognitive strategies, how to teach strategies, and what to do if they can't be taught. In M. Pressley & C. J. Brainerd (eds.), *Cognitive learning and memory in children: Progress in cognitive development research,* pp. 1–47. New York: Springer-Verlag.

Segal, J. W., Chipman, S. F. & Glaser, R. (1985). *Thinking and learning skills, Volume 1: Relating instruction to research.* Hillsdale, NJ: Erlbaum.

Chipman, S. F., Segal, J. W. & Glaser, R. (1985). *Thinking and learning skills, Volume 2: Research and open questions.* Hillsdale, NJ: Erlbaum.

Sternberg, R. J. (1985). *Beyond I.Q.: A triarchic theory of human intelligence.* NY: Cambridge University Press.

Practice

Adams, M. (Ed.) (1986). *Odyssey: A curriculum for thinking.* Watertown, MA: Mastery Education Corporation.

DeBono, E. (1983). *The CoRT Thinking Program.* New York: Pergamon Press.

Feuerstein, R. (1980). *Instrumental enrichment: An intervention program for cognitive modifiability.* Baltimore, MD: University Park Press.

Marzano, J. R. (1991). Tactics for thinking: A program for initiating the teaching of thinking. In A. Costa (Ed.), *Developing minds: Programs for teaching thinking, Volume 2.* Alexandria, Virginia: ASCD.

Perkins, D. N., Goodrich, H., Tishman, S., & Owen, J. M. (1994) *Thinking connections: Learning to think and thinking to learn.* California: Addison-Wesley.

Polya, G. (1957). *How to solve it: A new aspect of mathematical method* (2nd ed.). Garden City, NY: Doubleday.

Swartz., R. & Parks, S. (1994). *Infusing the teaching of critical and creative thinking into elementary instruction.* Pacific grove, CA: Critical thinking press and software.

Swartz., R. & Parks, S. (in press). *Infusing the teaching of critical and creative thinking into secondary instruction.* Pacific grove, CA: Critical thinking press and software.

Swartz, R. J. & Perkins, D. N. (1989). *Teaching thinking: Issues and approaches.* Pacific Grove, CA: Midwest Publications.

CHAPTERS 10 AND 11: HIGHER ORDER KNOWLEDGE

Theory

Collins, A. & Ferguson, W. (1993). Epistemic Forms and Epistemic Games. *Educational Psychologist, 28*(1), 25–42.

Ohlsson, S. (1993). Abstract schemas. *Educational Psychologist, 28*(1), 51–66.

Perkins, D. N., Jay, E., & Tishman, S. (1993). New conceptions of thinking: From ontology to education. *Educational Psychologist, 28*(1), 67–85.

Perkins, D. N. & Simmons, R. (1988). Patterns of misunderstanding: An integrative model of misconceptions in science, mathematics, and programming. *Review of Educational Research, 58*(3), 303–326.

Practice

Perkins, D. N. (1986). *Knowledge as design.* Hillsdale, NJ: Erlbaum.

Perkins, D. N. (1992). *Smart schools: From training memories to educating minds.* New York: The Free Press.

Lipman, M., Sharp, A., & Oscanyon, F. (1980). *Philosophy in the classroom.* Philadelphia: Temple University.

CHAPTERS 12 AND 13:
TEACHING FOR TRANSFER

Theory

Brown, A. L. (1989). Analogical learning and transfer: What develops? In S. Vosniadou & A. Ortony, eds. *Similarity and analogical reasoning*, pp. 369–412. New York: Cambridge University Press.

Cormier, S. M. & Hagman, J. D. (eds.) (1987) Transfer of learning: contemporary research and application. New York: Academic Press.

Royer, J. (1979). Theories of the transfer of learning. *Educational Psychologist 14*, 53–69.

Salomon, G. & Perkins, D. N. (1989). Rocky roads to transfer: Rethinking mechanisms of a neglected phenomenon. *Educational Psychologist, 24*(2), 113–142.

Practice

Fogarty, R., Perkins, D. N., and Barell, J. (1991). *How to teach for transfer.* Palatine, IL: Skylight Publishing.

Perkins, D. N. & Salomon, G. (1988). Teaching for transfer. *Educational Leadership, 46* (1), 22–32.